Semiotics in Language Education

Approaches to Applied Semiotics 2

Editor-in-Chief
Thomas A. Sebeok

Executive Editor
Jean Umiker-Sebeok

Mouton de Gruyter
Berlin · New York

Semiotics in Language Education

by
Marcel Danesi

Mouton de Gruyter
Berlin · New York 2000

Mouton de Gruyter (formerly Mouton, The Hague)
is a Division of Walter de Gruyter GmbH & Co. KG, Berlin

♾ Printed on acid-free paper which falls within the guidelines
of the ANSI to ensure permanence and durability.

Library of Congress Cataloging-in-Publication-Data

Danesi, Marcel, 1946—
    Semiotics in language education / by Marcel Danesi.
      p. cm. — (Approaches to applied semiotics)
    Includes bibliographical references and index.
    ISBN 3 11 016914 2 (alk. paper) —
    ISBN 3 11 016915 0 (pbk.: alk. paper)
        1. Language and languages — Study and teaching. 2. Se-
    miotics. 3. Language acquisition.
    I. Title.   II. Series.
    P53.774.D36 2000
    418'.0071—dc21
                                                    00-033862

Die Deutsche Bibliothek — *CIP-Einheitsaufnahme*

Danesi, Marcel:
Semiotics in language education / by Marcel Danesi. — Berlin ;
New York : Mouton de Gruyter, 2000
    (Approaches to applied semiotics ; 2)
    ISBN 3-11-016914-2 geb.
    ISBN 3-11-016915-0 brosch.

Printing: W. Hildebrand, Berlin.
Binding: Lüderitz & Bauer, Berlin.
Cover design: Christopher Schneider, Berlin.
Printed in Germany.

Preface

Students in high school, college, and university classrooms throughout the world customarily characterize their attempts to learn a new language as a monumental struggle, especially when they compare their efforts to how easily and *naturally* they were able to acquire their native language during infancy and childhood. Throughout the twentieth century, the question of why it is so difficult to master a *second language* in a classroom environment came to constitute a central preoccupation of language educators throughout the globe. Is there anything, they would constantly ask, that can be done *in the classroom* to make language learning less of a struggle, and more comparable to how the native language is acquired? Attempts to answer this question led to the founding of the discipline of *applied (educational) linguistics* which, during the last quarter of the century, developed into two branches known generally as *second language acquisition research* and *second language teaching methodology*.

The normal plan for resolving the problem of how to impart native-like fluency in the classroom was a relatively simple one; it consisted, basically, in extracting pedagogical principles from the scientific research on both *language* by linguists and on the *learner* by psychologists. These were then used to devise pedagogical practices and instructional materials that teachers were expected to adapt to their specific situations. The underlying assumption was that the degree of success of language learning was proportional to the degree to which the practices and materials were compatible with the prevailing linguistic and psychological theories, *regardless of who was doing the teaching*. But after a century of such practices, surveys continue to show that only a small fraction of all language students exposed to structured classroom instruction eventually achieve native-like proficiency. The vast majority of students, it would seem, are probably going to have to be content with learning approximations of the language, *no matter how they are taught it*.

As a teacher of Italian as a second language for over a quarter of a century, I too have been annoyed constantly by the many persistent difficulties that the classroom learning situation entails. As an instructor of semiotics during the same period of time, I started wondering a decade ago if the challenges posed by classroom language learning could be studied profitably from the particular perspective of semiotic theory. Thus, I embarked on a series of research projects whose results impressed upon me how powerful semiotics is as a framework for investigating classroom language behavior. I also found, to my surprise, that although much has been written on the education-semiotics interface, very little has been published on the relevance of semiotics to second language teaching. Hence, the reason for this book. I have written it as an introductory text for teachers, educators, applied linguists, and anyone else interested in the contribution that semiotics can make to language education. Even though the term *language education* will be used ordinarily in reference to *second language education* in classroom contexts, I believe that the ideas discussed in this book are applicable to language education generally (e.g. to bilingual models of education, to immersion education, etc.).

The opening chapter provides a brief historical analysis of the main trends in second language education in the twentieth century; the second introduces the notion of *network theory* and the semiotic principles upon which it is based; the third, fourth, and fifth chapters then deal respectively with *denotative, connotative,* and *metaphorical concepts*. Network theory is drafted to provide a framework for discussing student discourse in comparison with target culture discourse. It is based on the idea that concepts form associative connections based on sense and on inference.

I must warn readers from the outset about what not to expect from this book. First, they will not find in it an in-depth treatment of semiotics proper. Relevant works for further consultation in semiotic theory are listed in the bibliography at the back, which contains not only cited works, but also useful ones dealing with both semiotics and second language education. Second, they will not find a critical discussion of the purported advantages of one approach over another (e.g. a Saussurean vs. a Peircean approach to the sign). Finally, readers should also not expect to find a prescription of how to impart native-like fluency in a language to classroom language learners. Semiotics is useful only in providing helpful *insights,* not overarching *solutions* in education. I will, however, discuss in some detail the implications that network theory has for language pedagogy. Whether readers agree or disagree with any or all of my comments, it is my sincere hope that they will be stimulated by this book to know more about the semiotics-language education interface. That and that alone will have made the writing of this book worthwhile.

I would like to thank, above anyone else, my students at the Ontario Institute for Studies in Education, University of Toronto, and University of Lugano. Their critical responses to my teaching, along with the many enthusiastic classroom discussions I have had with them over the years, have encouraged me to write this manual for a broader audience. A special debt of gratitude goes out to Professors Thomas A. Sebeok and Jean Umiker-Sebeok of Indiana University for the unwavering support they have always given to my ideas, and for inviting me to synthesize them in book form.

Contents

Chapter I
Language teaching and semiotics

1. Introductory remarks

The great Russian psychologist Lev Vygotsky (1978: 51) once remarked that the "very essence of memory is that human beings actively remember with the help of signs". In these words can be detected a plea for establishing a connection between *semiotics*, "the science studying signs and sign systems", *learning theory* "the science investigating how signs are learned and remembered", and *education*, "the instructional practices employed to teach individuals how to control signs". Although important research on this connection has been conducted by semioticians throughout the twentieth century, rarely has Vygotsky's entreaty shaped the development of "mainstream" educational practices. Before considering what Vygotsky's plea would entail in the area of *second language* (SL) education, it is useful to take a brief look first at how SL educational practices evolved in the twentieth century. This will provide a backdrop to the discussion that will follow in the subsequent chapters of this book.

The term *second language learning* (SLL) refers to the learning of a language after the *first* or *native language* (NL). The latter process is referred to generally as *first* or *native language acquisition* (NLA). The term *acquisition*, rather than *learning*, is used to indicate that the NL process unfolds in a largely unconscious manner. Analogously, the term *second language acquisition* (SLA) has been coined to distinguish between unconscious and conscious processes in second language learning. This distinction will be used in this book only whenever it is relevant. Incidentally, the NL is often symbolized as L_1 and the SL as L_2 in the relevant pedagogical literature—a convention that will not be adopted here. *Second language teaching* (SLT) is used to refer to any form or manifestation of instructional behavior involving SLs. SLT may be a *private* concern (one teacher-for-one learner), as it is, for instance, in so-called *Berlitz* schools, or a *class-*

room-based process, as it is in high school, college, or university settings. Only the latter meaning will be intended in this book when the term SLT is used.

1.1 Language education in the twentieth century

Around the year 1880, a radical new view of language education emerged that spread quickly among teachers and educators. Motivated by the premise that effective classroom instruction should be carried out according to psychologically-valid principles of learning, it emerged in reaction to the prevailing eighteenth and nineteenth century practice known as *grammar-translation* pedagogy. The latter was so called because its identifying instructional characteristic was the presentation of grammatical information about the SL that learners were expected to assimilate on their own and then apply as best they could to translation tasks. The new perspective led to the crystallization of a grass-roots movement among teachers and educators, known as the *reform movement*. The premise that inspired the movement became such an entrenched one in the minds of teachers throughout the twentieth century—even today it is virtually impossible to think of SLT as anything but a scientifically-designed form of instruction grounded in some psychologically-testable theory of learning.

One of the primary goals of the early reformers was to systematize pedagogical practices on the basis of sound psychological theories of SLA. This led to the development of the *method notion* in SLT, i.e. to the idea that SLA could be nurtured successfully in classroom settings only if instruction was conducted *methodically* according to a psychologically-based "plan of attack". It was thought that this could be realized only with standardized instructional techniques and pedagogical resources designed specifically for the teacher to carry out the plan as practically and effectively as possible.

1.1.1 The direct method

The grammar-translation approach traces its roots to the medieval and early Renaissance periods, when only Latin and Greek were deemed worthy of formal study in European schools. The learning of vernacular languages was tied to a practical need, and was assumed to be best accomplished through direct contact with the native speakers of those languages. This "social immersion" perspective of language learning, which McArthur (1983: 94) characterizes as the "marketplace" view of SLA, is actually the oldest learning theory in history, espoused by such ancient peoples as the Sumerians and the Babylonians (Titone 1968).

Latin was taught in a straightforward *deductive* way: teachers first presented a rule of grammar, after which they assigned oral and written translation tasks to students to test their ability to apply the rule. As the social and educational functions of Latin came to be assumed more and more by *vernacular* languages in the sixteenth century (from Latin *vernaculus* 'domestic, native'), the formal study of these languages started to take on increasing educational importance. From the outset, it was assumed that the teaching of vernacular languages was to be carried out with the same basic grammar-translation procedure that was used to teach the Classical languages (Titone 1968; Kelly 1969). Discovering that this approach was largely ineffectual when employed to teach communication skills in the vernacular languages, a group of educators proposed introducing some of the flavor of the "marketplace approach" into the classroom. Prominent among them were Guarino Guarini (1374-1460), St. Ignatius of Loyola (1491-1556), and Wolfgang Ratke (1571-1635), all of whom stressed the need for the grammar of the new language to be learned through induction, rather than rule-application to translation texts. After all, they argued, that is how children learned to speak and how the ability to communicate is acquired in the marketplace. In the seventeenth century, Jan Komensky, the Protestant bishop of Moravia, better known by his Latin name Comenius (1592-1670), also emphasized induction-oriented pedagogy, rather than grammar-translation. Comenius developed the technique of *situational dialoguing* so that students could induce the appropriate forms of language before they were taught explicitly to them.

Despite the efforts of such radical educators, the grammar-translation view of teaching vernacular languages prevailed right up to the late nineteenth century. Like Guarini, St. Ignatius, Ratke, and Comenius before them, the early reformers saw inductive learning as the *natural* mode of SLA. To this effect, they proposed transforming classroom instruction into a methodical approach that simulated the inductive processes guiding NLA. The linguist Henry Sweet (1899), for instance, made the explicit claim that SLT should be conceived as a pre-planned set of routines based on a scientific analysis of the target language and on a study of developmental psychology. In this way, he suggested, it would be possible for the SL teacher to select what was to be taught in a more effective manner, to know better what the limits of learning were, and to be in a better position to arrange the items to be taught in a coherent and psychologically-meaningful way.

Without delving into the complex socio-historical factors that converged at the turn of the century to install the method notion into the mindset of language educators, suffice it to say here that it coincided with four crucial events: (1) the emergence of linguistics as a science and, therefore, of a new focus on language as system; (2) the publication of the first psychological findings on how languages were purportedly learned and on how these can be employed to pedagogical advantage (Gouin 1880; Viëtor 1886; Sweet 1899; Jespersen 1904); (3) the foundation of the Modern Language Association of America in 1883 and of the Modern Language Association of Great Britain in 1889, both of which focused attention on the importance of the teaching process itself; and (4) the establishment of the International Phonetic Association in 1886, which drew awareness to the importance of accurate speech in language learning. The convergence of these events led to the rejection of grammar-translation practices in SLT and to the elaboration of the first modern inductive teaching method, called the *direct method*, which attained instant official recognition in France and Germany despite misgivings expressed by certain educators, and which was widely adopted in England and the United States.

The direct method came with its own teaching *syllabus*—a sequentially-organized compendium of structures that the instructor was to teach in the given succession—and textbook containing dialogues and pattern practice materials as the basis for classroom instruction (Richards and Rodgers 1986: 7-8). For the first time in the history of SLT in school, it was thought not only desirable but possible to give instructional practices a structure and a substance that would activate the student's natural learning mode and, thus, lead to profitable results.

The direct method was, in actual fact, the best known and more widely-used of the so-called *natural methods*, which included the ones of Saveur and Berlitz (Titone 1968: 100-101; Richards and Rodgers 1986: 9-10). The aim of all the natural methods was to simulate the conditions and processes that were thought to undergird NLA in the form and content of the teaching syllabus. For this reason, they amalgamated the use of demonstration, concrete association, pattern practice, imitation, and other procedures and routines into a format that was to be followed by teachers and textbook authors systematically. Although it is true that some of these had historical parallels—e.g. pattern practice drills were traceable to the substitution tables of sixteenth- and seventeenth-century grammars, situational dialogues originated in antiquity and were fine-tuned by Comenius, etc.—never before were they organized within the framework of a specific psychological perspective: SLA = NLA. To put it in contemporary figurative terms, the natural methods designed their "teaching software" on the basis of what was thought to be the student's natural "learning hardware". The way in which it interrelated the language, the teacher, the learner, the classroom situation, and the actions that take place within it changed SLT pedagogical practices in a permanent way. Indeed, many of the direct method's features and techniques continue to be used to this day (whether or not it is known) in a variety of pedagogical approaches.

1.1.2 The reading and oral methods

The first true scientific debate on the validity of the method notion was kindled by the publication in 1917 of Harold Palmer's groundbreaking theoretical treatment of the SLA-SLT interface. Palmer stressed, above all else, that SLT should be more adaptive to the particular needs of the students. Rather than develop a single, standardized format to teach all students, as the congeners of the direct method envisaged, teachers should base their classroom practices, Palmer submitted, on how much material their students could actually absorb. By the early 1920s disenchantment with the direct method had grown considerably. As Palmer suspected, it turned out that the psychological theory on which it was based, namely that SLA = NLA, was not reflective of all aspects of SLA, nor were all the pedagogical principles that it had fostered applicable to all classroom situations.

With the demise of the direct method a new debate was ignited between inductivists and deductivists. From this, two new and highly influential methods—the *reading* and the *oral methods*—emerged. The former grew out of the widely-held view in the 1920s that the only realistically-attainable goal in a non-immersion learning environment was reading comprehension. Like the grammar-translation approach of previous centuries, the originators of the *reading method* stressed the role of grammar instruction in the native language of the learner. But, like the direct method architects, they also stressed proper pronunciation (which was regarded as an indispensable aid to comprehension) and the need to formulate explanations of grammar in terms of a scientific analysis of the target language. They introduced into the general practice of SLT the highly useful notions of controlled vocabulary learning and of graded readers. The reading method continues to be used in modified form to this day, because, as a grammar-translation approach, it makes few demands on teachers, and therefore continues to have considerable appeal in situations where the primary goal of SL study is the reading of literary texts. As Richards and Rodgers (1986: 5) have aptly remarked, it is used today by people trained in literary criticism rather than in applied linguistics or SLA theory; consequently, while it "is still widely practiced, it has no advocates", because it is a method "for which there is no theory".

The *oral method* was developed by British linguists in the 1930s. It was a truly innovative proposal at the time. Indeed, many of its techniques continue to be used today by many textbook authors and syllabus designers. It stressed a strict control over vocabulary, a grading of grammatical items from simple to complex, the oral presentation of new material (hence the name *oral method*), the introduction of reading and writing after it could be determined that a sufficient lexical and grammatical competence was developed by students, the exclusive use of the SL in the classroom, and the situational practice of new notions and structures. Its practice of presenting new material to reflect real-life situations made it highly popular with teachers (Halliday, McIntosh and Strevens (1964: 38). The teaching syllabus, which graded grammatical structures from simple to complex, came a little later to be known as the *structural syllabus*.

1.1.3 The audiolingual and audiovisual methods

By the 1940s and 1950s, disenchantment starting growing with both the reading and oral methods. Once again, as Palmer had suspected about the method notion itself, they were not applicable to every learning situation. Nevertheless, educators of the era did not abandon the aspiration of developing a "universal" method for SLT that would be applicable to all situations. Two developments convinced them that this was within their reach. First, the *behaviorist movement* in psychology provided a new theory of language learning, based on habit formation, that could easily be translated into instructional practices (Bloomfield 1942). Second, the unparalleled success of the so-called *Army specialized training program*, which was designed for army members during World War II on behaviorist principles, suggested that its basic pedagogical plan—the use of imitation, repetition, and dialogue practice stages—was the "panacea" for which teachers had been searching since the reform movement.

These inspired the creation of a new method—the *audiolingual method*—which was heralded in America as the "method to end all methods". It stressed habit-formation, pattern practice, and inductive training procedures. It also rejected the SLA = NLA hypothesis, adopting the view that the stored NL knowledge possessed by learners greatly determined the ways in which they perceived and assimilated the new language. As the linguist Charles Fries (1927, 1945) argued, the motivation for this new view of SLA—known as *transfer theory*—grew out of the common observations of classroom teachers that the pronunciation habits and the grammatical and lexical categories of the NL were unconsciously transferred to the learning of the SL, especially during the initial stages. The technique called *contrastive analysis* was developed from this view. By contrasting the structures of the target and native languages, it was thought possible to determine what areas of pronunciation, grammar would require more emphasis and what areas would not. Those in which NL habits and grammatical categories coincided with SL ones would receive less emphasis because the transfer process—known as *positive transfer*—would allow the students to acquire them unconsciously; those in which they differed would instead receive more emphasis because the transfer process in this case—known as *negative transfer*—would interfere with the acquisition process.

In Europe, the success of the army *program* was translated into a slightly different method that came to be called the *audiovisual method*, developed in the 1950s in France at the *Centre du recherche et d'étude pour la diffusion du français*. The method was very similar in pedagogical design to its American counterpart, stressing pattern practice, habit formation, and the teaching of oral skills before reading and writing skills. But it added an innovative feature to this basic plan—the new material was to be presented visually with filmstrips.

The enthusiastic expectations that both these methods raised were heightened by a naive faith in technology. The incorporation of the "language laboratory" into the *modus operandi* of the audiolingual method, and of visual aids into that of the audiovisual method, were hailed by many teachers at the time as the final missing pieces to the puzzle of what had be done in the classroom to instill true mastery of the SL into the learner. But their enthusiasm turned into disenchantment as a series of events and experiences coalesced by the mid-1960s to bring about the large-scale abandonment of both methods. For one thing, the expectations raised by the two methods were never fulfilled in practice. Moreover, by the 1960s the psychological and linguistic platform upon which they were constructed crumbled under the weight of a new emphasis on *cognitivism* in psychology (Ausubel 1967) and *generativism* in linguistics (Chomsky 1957, 1965). A series of psycholinguistic experiments moreover—especially the one by Scherer and Wertheimer (1964)—showed that no significant learning outcomes were produced by these methods, when compared to grammar-translation approaches.

1.1.4 The cognitive-code method

Based in large part on the theoretical notions of generative linguistics, a new method emerged in the early 1970s, called the *cognitive-code method*, which was designed by applied linguists (e.g. Jakobovits 1971; Chastain 1971; Lugton 1971). The pedagogical outlook of this method was grounded on the notion of *linguistic competence*—namely, that knowing a language consisted in knowing its basic rules of grammatical design. It was thus formatted to provide learning materials and exercises designed to impart knowledge of abstract rules of language organization. However, the method never really "caught on" with teachers at large, so to speak, and was abandoned by the mid-1970s.

The applied linguists of that decade also introduced a new technique into SLT that continues to be used profitably to this day. Known as *error analysis*, it was based on the observation that the kind of competence that students typically manifest as they speak and write—called *interlanguage*—was characterized above all else by predictable, recurring errors (Selinker 1972; Richards 1974; Ludwig 1979; Corder 1981; Robinett and Schachter 1983). *Errors* were distinguished from *mistakes*. The latter were the many blunders that students make but which they can easily correct themselves; the former, instead, revealed gaps in linguistic competence.

Error analyses of student interlanguages made it obvious that there are two main types of errors committed by learners: (1) *interlinguistic*, which are caused by interferences from the NL, i.e. by the negative transfer of some habit or category from the NL to the SL; and (2) *intralinguistic*, which are caused by the same learning mechanisms that characterize NLA, i.e. by generalization, analogy, simplification, etc. Interlanguage theorists claimed that the systematicity and predictability of errors showed that learners typically construct a "working theory" of the SL grammar that is based on certain general principles of language design extrapolated from the input to which they have been exposed.

1.1.5 The communicative language teaching movement

The primary goal of the direct, reading, audiolingual, and audiovisual methods was to provide an appropriate structural syllabus and a specific instructional plan for imparting linguistic competence in a sequential, organized way. The ability to apply the SL structures to real-life communicative situations was assumed to emerge spontaneously after they had been acquired. The only true dissenting voice in this scenario was that of the creators of the oral method (above

§1.1.2). In the other methods, the oral dialogical input was controlled primarily for its structural content; i.e. although it was meant to simulate real-life conversation, it was so watered down and scripted to follow the sequence of structures in the syllabus that it hardly ever resembled real discourse.

In the early 1970s, the linguist Dell Hymes (1972) challenged the idea of linguistic competence as abstract grammatical knowledge that was impervious to influences from real-world communication and social interaction. He proposed that knowledge of language structure was interconnected with knowledge of how to use it appropriately in specific social settings. He called this interconnection *communicative competence.* Hymes' notion held an instant appeal to teachers, who at the time were also beginning to suspect that the method notion was fundamentally flawed, since it entailed the artificial study of language as a code, separate from its uses. This led to a true paradigm shift in language education—as the philosopher Thomas Kuhn (1970) called a radical change in philosophical outlook—which, in turn, led to the *communicative language teaching movement.* This lasted throughout the 1970s and 1980s.

The first steps to develop *communicative syllabi* to replace the previous structural ones were taken by the Council of Europe. Already by the mid-1970s two highly influential syllabi, called the *threshold level* (Van Ek 1975) and the *notional-functional syllabus* (Wilkins 1976), emerged. The organizing principle in both was the concept of *speech act*, defined as a communicative strategy that native speakers employ unconsciously to carry out specific types of social interactions. A simple protocol like saying *hello*, for instance, constitutes a speech act that requires a detailed knowledge of the appropriate words, phrases, structures, and nonverbal cues that come together cohesively in a script-like fashion to enable a speaker to make successful social contact with another speaker. An infringement of any of the procedural details of this script might lead to a breakdown in communication, or worse, to confrontation. Drawing upon the ideas of linguists like Firth (1957) and Halliday (1973, 1975) and philosophers like Austin (1962) and Searle (1969), the early architects of communicative syllabi tailored the structural information pertaining to SL grammar and vocabulary in their syllabi to reflect its uses in speech situations.

1.1.6 The humanistic language teaching movement

The 1970s and 1980s also witnessed a second shift in SLT philosophy, known generally as *humanistic language teaching*, that, however, never became part of the SL educational mainstream. The humanistic movement provided, essentially, an alternative to communicative language teaching. It was motivated by the conviction, expressed almost sixty years earlier by Palmer, that the personality characteristics and emotional needs of the students were of paramount importance in guaranteeing successful SLA. The most widely-discussed (more so than widely-used) humanistic methods were Curran's *community counseling* (1976), Gattegno's *silent way* (1976), Asher's *total physical response* (1977, 1981), Lozanov's *suggestopedia* (1979), Krashen and Terrell's *natural approach* (1983), and Di Pietro's *scenario approach* (1987). Despite considerable differences in approach and in the techniques used, all these shared three central beliefs: (1) the need to provide a non-threatening and congenial learning environment; (2) the need to get students involved directly in the learning process; and (3) the need to establish a climate of amicability between teacher and students. The founders of these methods consistently reported profitable results. The reason for their success, however, did not require any great leap of the imagination—a learner who feels comfortable and a contributing participant in the learning process is bound to acquire skills more easily. The main drawback of the humanistic methods was that they required the teacher's total commitment to their specific instructional script, leaving very little leeway for extemporization and teacher creativity. For this reason, they never really caught on with the language teaching profession at large.

Nevertheless, they have been pivotal in pointing out the importance of taking the student's emotional needs into direct account in SLT. Among the important pedagogical inferences that can be drawn for language learning theory from the humanistic movement, the following stand out:

- The greatest obstacle to learning a language is, as Curran assumed, the anxiety the learner experiences in the traditional language class.

- As Gattegno emphasized, the more the teacher talks and explains, the less the learner is likely to learn. Hence the need for the teacher to give students more opportunities to express themselves.

- With that exact same goal in mind, Di Pietro went so far as to assign to the students themselves the task of giving the content of the course its specific shape, allowing them to invent their own verbal strategies for handling real-life happenings. He saw the teacher's role as that of an adviser and guide, explaining aspects of grammar and vocabulary as needed.

- Asher reemphasized what the direct methodologists knew all to well, namely that learning outcomes are enhanced when the target language is associated with physical actions. For this reason, Asher stressed that new material be introduced through commands to which students must respond physically (*Open the door! Show me where the eraser is!* etc.).

- Lozanov introduced the idea that the potential for long-term learning is increased considerably if conditions are created in the classroom that are capable of activating subliminal (unconscious) processes—i.e. learning without the students realizing it.

- Taking their cue from this idea, Krashen introduced the distinction between *acquisition* (unconscious) and *learning* (conscious) processes in SLT. At first, both Krashen and Terrell claimed that grammar training was virtually useless as a pedagogical technique, since they believed that knowledge of structure would emerge spontaneously through an inbuilt "monitoring" system. But before his untimely death in 1991, Terrell modified this view somewhat. Acquisition is defined as a largely unconscious process that occurs within and outside the classroom spontaneously; learning, on the other hand, is defined a conscious process based on the monitoring of the input to which a student is exposed in a classroom situation.

1.1.7 The second language teaching dilemma

By the mid-1980s, general SLT practices became much more flexible and less "trendy", as teachers and educators sought diverse ways to understand SLA in classroom environments. The *proficiency movement* in the United States, for example, led to much discussion and interesting spin-off research on how to integrate structural and communicative syllabi (e.g. Omaggio 1986, Schulz 1986). However, as they enter the twenty-first century, teachers may know a lot more about the nature of linguistic and communicative competence, and about learning theories and learner needs, than did their nineteenth century predecessors, but paradoxically they still face the same annoying dilemma that the reformers attempted to solve with the establishment of the direct method. For the sake of convenience it will be called the *SLT dilemma*: Why is it that after studying a language for varying periods of time, students still seem to lack the ability to speak with the same kind of "naturalness" that is instantly detectable in native-speaker discourse? As students speak or write it is quite apparent that, with few exceptions, there is an incongruity between the *surface structure* of their discourse, consisting of SL words and sentences, and its *conceptual underlying structure*.

The claim of this book is that the source of the "unnaturalness" evident in student discourse can be traced to the student's inability to interconnect the surface and conceptual levels of language. In this book, the ability to control surface structure will be called *verbal fluency*; and the ability to interconnect this level with its underlying conceptual structure will instead be called *conceptual fluency*. A large part of the empirical work in applied linguistics and SLA research in the twentieth century attempted to resolve the SLT dilemma by focusing on verbal fluency, i.e. by focusing on linguistic and communicative competence. The objective of the remainder of this book is to focus instead on of conceptual fluency and to describe the *semiotic competence* that undergirds it. Semiotic competence can be defined simply as the ability to interconnect verbal and conceptual structures in speech in culturally-appropriate ways.

1.2 Language acquisition

Only sporadically in the literature produced by the various movements discussed above is there a mention of *semiotics*, although there have been a number of works dealing with various aspects of semiosis, verbal and nonverbal, in language education (Kress 1995; Sebeok 1991a). Therefore, before discussing conceptual fluency, it is essential to look over rapidly some of the key semiotic notions related to native and second language acquisition, so as to establish a frame of reference for the discussion to follow.

Particularly useful in understanding language acquisition is the notion of *semiosis*—the innate ability of the brain and the sensory systems to produce and comprehend *signs*. *Representation*, on the other hand, is learned behavior. It entails the ability to represent things, ideas, events, etc. in ways with the signs provided by a specific culture. In the case of language acquisition, semiosis dominates the initial neonate period of development. When infants come into contact with unfamiliar objects, their instinctive reaction is to explore them with the *senses*, i.e. to handle them, taste them, smell them, listen to any sounds they make, and visually observe their features. This exploratory semiosic phase constitutes a *sensory knowing* stage—a stage that the Swiss psychologist Jean Piaget (1923, 1936, 1945, 1990) called appropriately a *sensory-motor stage*.

During this sensory phase infants are capable of distinguishing meaningful environmental stimuli (such as verbal ones) from random noises and of exploring the world around them with all their senses. The mental images that result from sensory knowing allow infants to *recognize* the same objects subsequently without having, each time, to examine them over again thoroughly with their sensory modalities. Now, as infants grow, they start to engage more and more in semiosic behavior that displaces this sensory phase; i.e. they start pointing to the object and imitating the sounds it makes, rather than just handling it, tasting it, etc. These imitations and indications are the child's first attempts at *representing* the world (Morris 1938, 1946). Piaget called this the *pre-operational stage*, since it is during this phase that children are able to operate certain tasks involving previously-formed sensory concepts. Thereafter, the repertoire of representational activities increases dramatically, as children learn more and more how to refer to the world through the system of signs to which they have been exposed in cultural context. From that point on, *sensory knowing* yields to *conceptual knowing*. From the age of 7-11 years, which Piaget called the *concrete operations stage*, children become sophisticated representers of the world.

Language is a representational device that allows children to re-place sensory modes of knowing with conceptual ones. At the same time that children learn to use language as a representational device, they are also learning in tandem how to use other such devices— pictorial, musical, etc. The ability to interconnect these different aspects of representation is what constitutes *semiotic competence*.

1.2.1 Native language acquisition

The scientific study of NLA is a relatively recent academic enter-prise, dating back only to the latter years of the nineteenth century. The three main historical periods into which this field of investiga-tion is generally subdivided are as follows: (1) the *diary period* (1876-1926), a period marked by the use of diaries or biographical annotations of an individual child's daily verbal development; (2) the *behaviorist period* (1926-1957), an era characterized by the system-atic observations of the verbal behavior manifested by children se-lected at random from a population; (3) the *longitudinal period* (1957-present), a period typified by the study of cases of language development over long stretches of time.

The research has shown that the patterns characterizing NLA are largely predictable across cultures. This led the linguist Noam Chomsky in the 1960s to claim that human infants possess a species-specific capacity to develop their native-language grammars by simply being exposed to verbal input. The human brain, Chomsky suggested, must have a special device for detecting and reproducing language. He called it a *language acquisition device*. In the 1980s, he then went on to propose the existence of another innate feature of the brain—a *universal grammar* (e.g. Chomsky 1986, 1990)—which he described as a set of universal principles of language design that are constrained by the specific *parameters* that characterize the grammar of the specific language to which the child is exposed.

As with any overarching theory of language, there are many problems with such universalist ideas. These will not be dealt with here for they are subsidiary to the main purpose at hand. For one thing, as Jacobs (1988: 330) aptly puts it, any theory of language acquisition "will have to consider what the environment brings to the brain, including both the input itself (e.g. structure, intonation, morphology) and the surrounding situational variables (e.g. gestures, discourse context); and, just as importantly, must also consider what the brain does to this information". A second problem is that universal grammar theory assigns a unique status to the language faculty in human development. The question of whether or not it is part of a larger semiosic capacity that is also responsible for the development of musical, humor, and other nonverbal faculties is largely discarded by proponents of this theory.

Theoretical quibbling aside, the studies have shown that, despite considerable individual variation in the rate of the developmental process and in the order of acquisition of the specific traits of a language, children all over the world follow a similar path on the way to speech, often called *acquisition by stages* (Weir 1962; Miller and Ervin 1964; Lenneberg 1967; Brown 1973). Among the first to document this process was the semiotician Roman Jakobson (1941). Jakobson found that children learned typically to use phonemes (minimal units of distinctive sound) to refer to objects and events in their immediate environment by first distinguishing between general phonic categories (e.g. consonants vs. vowels) and then by further discriminating among the significant differences within each category—known as progressive *phonemic differentiation*. Phonemic distinctions are perceived by the hearing center of the brain and produced through its motor pathways via a complex neural coordination system. There are twelve cranial nerves. Seven of these link the brain with the vocal organs. Some perform a motor function, controlling the movement of muscles; while others perform a sensory function, sending signals to the brain. The larynx controls the flow of air to and from the lungs, so as to prevent food, foreign objects, or other substances from entering the trachea on their way to the stomach. The ability to control the vocal folds makes it possible to build up pressure within the lungs and to emit air not only for expiration purposes, but also for the production of sound.

The research on NLA has, since Jakobson's pivotal work, established certain milestones in verbal development. These can be synthesized as follows. After an initial cooing stage that starts virtually at birth, around six months children begin babbling and eventually imitating the linguistic sounds they hear in the immediate environment. These imitations lead to the first words, which are monosyllabic reductions of adult words—*ma* for *mama*, *da* for *dog*, *ca* for *cat*, etc. These constitute the first acts of conceptual, rather than pure sensory, knowing. At eight months reduplications and imitative repetitions become more frequent in child discourse. Moreover, children start employing intonation patterns distinctly to convey emphasis and emotional states. By the end of the first year, the first true words emerge (*mama, dada*, etc.). In the 1960s, the psychologist Martin Braine (1963, 1971) noticed that these single words gradually embodied the communicative functions of entire phrases: e.g. the child's word *dada* could mean "Where is daddy"? "I want daddy", etc. according to situation. He called them *holophrastic*, or one-word, utterances. In situations of normal upbringing, holophrases reveal that a vast amount of conceptual development has taken place in the child by the end of the first year of life. During the holophrastic stage, in fact, children can name objects, express actions or the desire to carry out actions, and transmit emotional states rather effectively (Cruttenden 1974; Schwartz, Leonard, Wilcox, and Folger 1980).

Holophrases are the result of imitation. But the imitation deployed is hardly pure mimicry. It is a creative form of simulation that semioticians call *iconicity* (chapter 2, §2.2.1). Over 60% will develop into nouns, and 20% will become verbs. In a study of four infants from different language backgrounds, Boysson-Bardies and Vihman (1991) found that the actual forms and functions that holophrases take depend on developmental physiological constraints and on the specific language input to which a child is exposed. The early holo-phrases are, in effect, the semiosic products of the child's attempts to transform sensory states of knowing into conceptual ones. By 16-18 months, the child starts manifesting a remarkable ability to employ holophrastic language creatively. As Vygotsky (1961: 298) aptly put it: "The primary word is not a straightforward symbol for a concept but rather an image, a picture, a mental sketch of a short concept, a short tale about it—indeed, a small work of art".

During the second year, the child's ability to use intonation in-creases rapidly, reaching adult norms (Weeks (1982). At about 18-24 months, the child then passes on to what Braine (1971) called the *telegraphic stage*—a stage characterized by two- and three-word ut-terances. He called it *telegraphic* because, like composing a tele-gram, children construct their utterances in a condensed fashion, without all the elements that characterize adult syntax: *More milk, Daddy home*, etc. Braine characterized their organization as reflec-tive of a "pivot grammar", given that some of the words functioned as grammatical pivots (*more, less*, etc.) while others belonged to a more open lexical class (*milk, candy*, etc.). Around this pivot gram-mar the acquisition of vocabulary increases dramatically and rapidly. As children enter this stage, they have knowledge of about 270 words. By the age of 4-5, they can manage thousands of words.

The NLA process is completed, according to most psycholo-gists, around puberty. That is the period during which language is said to have been completely *lateralized* to the left hemisphere (LH) of the brain in most individuals. The discovery that language is con-trolled by the LH is traced back to 1861 when the French anthro-pologist and surgeon Paul Broca noticed a destructive lesion in the left frontal lobe during the autopsy of a patient who had lost the abil-ity to articulate words during his lifetime, even though he had not suffered any paralysis of his speech organs. Broca concluded that the capacity to articulate speech was traceable to that specific cerebral site—which shortly thereafter came to bear his name (*Broca's Area*). This discovery established a direct connection between a semiosic capacity and a specific area of the brain. Broca also discovered that there existed an *asymmetry* between the brain and the body by showing that right-handed persons were more likely to have language located in the LH.

In 1874 the work of the German neurologist Carl Wernicke brought to the attention of the medical community further evidence linking the LH with language. Wernicke documented cases in which damage to another area of the LH—which came to bear his name (*Wernicke's Area*)—consistently produced a recognizable pattern of impairment to the faculty of speech comprehension. Then, in 1892 Jules Déjerine showed that problems in reading and writing resulted primarily from damage to the LH alone. So, by the end of the nineteenth century the research evidence that was accumulating provided an empirical base to the emerging consensus in neuroscience that the LH was the cerebral locus for language. Unfortunately, it also contributed to the unfounded idea that the RH (right hemisphere) was without special functions and subject to the control of the so-called "dominant" LH.

Right after Wernicke's observations, the notion of *cerebral dominance*, or the idea that the LH is the dominant one in the higher forms of cognition, came to be a widely-held one in neuroscience. Although the origin of this term is obscure, it grew no doubt out of the research connecting language to the LH and out of the cultural link in Western society between language and the higher mental functions. It took the research in neuroscience most of the first half of the twentieth century to dispel the notion that only the verbal part of the brain was the crucial one for generating the higher forms of cognition, and to establish the fact that the brain is structured anatomically and physiologically in such a way as to provide for two modes of thinking, the verbal and the nonverbal.

It was during the 1950s and 1960s that the widely-publicized studies conducted by the American psychologist Roger Sperry (e.g. 1968, 1973) and his associates on epilepsy patients who had had their two hemispheres separated by surgical section showed that both hemispheres, not just a dominant one, were needed in a neurologically-cooperative way to produce complex thinking. In the 1970s the research in neuroscience suggested, moreover, that for any new verbal input to be comprehensible, it must occur in contexts that allow the synthetic functions of the RH to do their interpretive work first.

In effect, it showed that the brain is prepared to interpret new information primarily in terms of its contextual characteristics.

Today, neuroscientists have at their disposal a host of truly remarkable technologies for mapping and collecting data on brain functioning. The use of *positron emission tomography* (PET brain scanning), for instance, has become a particularly powerful investigative tool for neuroscientists, since it provides images of mental activities such as those that produce language.

1.2.2 Second language acquisition

The two main theories of SLA before the communicative language teaching movement were: (1) the SLA = NLA theory of the direct methodologists and (2) the transfer theory developed by audiolingual methodologists. A third theory, called *interdependence theory*, which came forward in the early 1960s, seemed to strike a middle ground between these two contrasting viewpoints. It was formulated in 1962 by psychologists Peal and Lambert who argued that the native and second language systems were *interdependent* components of a global language competence. They suggested that the two language codes have both divergent and overlapping functions, meanings, and forms. The learner will thus tend to fill-in the gaps in areas of divergence with NL categories. This would explain the ephemeral interferences that surface during the student's initial attempts to speak and write the SL. However, through the gaining of proficiency the common core comes to form a cognitive basis for verbal skill transfer, eventually putting the learner in a position to recognize language differences consciously and, therefore, to separate them cognitively and functionally (see also Cummins 1979, 1984).

A few years later, in 1967, the linguist Eric Lenneberg claimed that the *critical period* for language lateralization was from birth to about puberty. Shortly after Lenneberg's book came out, and gained widespread renown, its implications for SLA simply could not be overlooked. If it were in fact true that the acquisition of language after the critical period posed a monumental, if not impossible, neurological task, then presumably there was nothing teachers could do. But Lenneberg's *critical period hypothesis* produced just the opposite reaction, spurring on SL teachers and SLA researchers even

more so to find a suitable theory of SLA and thus solve the SLT dilemma once and for all (Krashen 1973, 1975).

The two main questions that researchers tried to answer in the
post-Lenneberg era were the following ones: (1) Is SLA characterized by stages? (2) If so, are the stages that characterize NLA and
SLA different, parallel, or complementary? From the research on interlanguages it became immediately apparent that errors tend to form
a sequential pattern. This suggested to some that there exists a *natural order* to SLA by which certain structures are acquired early and
others later on. This implied, further, that fluency in the SL cannot be
taught but must emerge naturally, once learners have developed linguistic competence through understanding the input to which they
have been exposed. In line with this general finding, emphasis in
SLT was put in the 1980s on ensuring that the input to which students are exposed is designed to follow the supposed natural order in
terms of its complexity. *Stage models* of SLA were also developed so
that teaching practices could be based on the natural order hypothesis
(Obler 1980; Galloway and Krashen 1980; Krashen 1985; Gass and
Madden 1985).

The fact remains, however, that such models have not solved the
SLT dilemma by any stretch of the imagination. People seem to learn
second languages more successfully when they become immersed in
the cultures of the communities that speak them than they do by being exposed to input structured according to stages. The reason for
this, actually, has a straightforward semiotic explanation—learning a
language in its natural cultural context allows the learner to interrelate its forms and uses to the broader *signifying order* to which it is
tied.

Each language is designed to encode concepts in different ways.
The more distant the relation between languages, the greater the conceptual differences between them. Although people with different
languages may see the same *rainbow* in the same way, the number
and range of the rainbow's *hues* they can name will depend on how
many color terms have been coded by their language. Some languages have everyday words for a dozen colors; other languages can
get by with only a couple. Languages leave uncoded that which has
been considered unimportant historically to a culture. For example,
nomadic Canadian Inuit had little interest in distinguishing different

types of trees; what they needed were words to talk about snow. In some Inuit dialects, therefore, more than 50 words referring to ice and snow are in use.

1.3 Semiotics and language education

The semiotic view of language as an representational device inter-connected with the other representational devices of a culture has not as yet penetrated the mindset of SLA researchers, probably because its general implications for language learning and for discourse pro-gramming have not been thoroughly examined. But, in the same way that teachers have gained specific insights from psychological and linguistic research in the past, so too can concrete pedagogical in-sights be gleaned from semiotic research.

Some interesting work has already been carried in what can be called *applied educational semiotics*, or simply *applied semiotics*. I mention, for the sake of historical accuracy, the pivotal research con-ducted in the late 1970s on the use of semiotic theory in SLT at the Research Center for Language and Semiotic Studies at Indiana Uni-versity, under the directorship of Thomas A. Sebeok. From that proj-ect a handbook on nonverbal communication for teachers of Japa-nese was published, which was accompanied by a widely used half-hour film in which native Japanese speakers were seen to execute culturally-appropriate gestures in tandem with conversational inter-actions (see Johnson 1979; Wintsch 1979; Tsuda 1984). This made it saliently obvious to teachers how intrinsically interconnected the gestural and verbal modes of signification are in the act of message delivery. Then, Harrison (1983) published a parallel handbook com-paring Brazilian and North American body language; and Rector and Trinta (1985) produced an illustrated manual on nonverbal commu-nication in Brazil.

In the 1980s and 1990s, semiotic ideas and notions were used implicitly in a series of studies describing the role of "body lan-guage" and gesture in SLT (e.g. Wiener, Shilkert, and Devoe 1980; Raffler-Engel 1980; Arndt and Pesch 1984; Morain 1986; Poyatos 1989; Diadori 1990). These studies provided evidence that teachers were beginning to feel intuitively the need to interrelate the verbal with the nonverbal dimension into teaching practices. As Wiener,

Shilkert, and Devoe (1980: 275) aptly remarked, "in stressing the importance of verbal communication", SLT methodologists in the past "seem also to have assumed the unimportance of nonverbal communication". The challenge for SLT that Sebeok posed in the mid-1980s (1985: 179) is worth reiterating here:

> If, as is the case, we lavish incalculable amounts of energy, time, and money to instill in children and adults a range of foreign language competencies, why are the indissolubly parallel foreign gesticulatory skills all but universally neglected, especially considering that even linguists are fully aware that what has been called the total communication package, best likened to a coaxial cable carrying many messages at the same time, is hardly an exaggerated simile?

The above studies have shown rather persuasively that gestures, body language, and other nonverbal dimensions of communication constitute a "cultural grammar" that should be taught in class as explicitly as are the rules of linguistic grammar and rehearsed as regularly as grammar. Videotaping native speakers in conversational settings, listing the proxemic and haptic rules that are appropriate for the students to learn in specific situations, and then role-playing conversations with appropriate body language can all be incorporated into the *modus operandi* of SLT. Role-playing situations in particular can easily be imagined to give the students exposure to, and practice in, nonverbal forms of communication.

In an informal pedagogical experiment I conducted in 1994, I found that students related easily to instruction in nonverbal communication and that they could learn aspects of culturally-appropriate body language as easily as they learned the various structures of verbal communication. Two classes of first-year non-credit Italian students at the University of Toronto were taught with the same teaching materials and communicative syllabus. The difference between the two classes was that in one case the instructor was given a pre-prepared manual and videotape showing appropriate Italian bodily postures, interpersonal contact rituals, gestures, facial expressions, handshake patterns, etc. that are characteristic of specific conversational settings. The manual also contained suggestions for role-playing activities. At the end of the course, the two groups of students were videotaped as they took part in simulated conversational interactions. The students in both groups were *not* instructed to use body language. They were simply told to role-play various scenarios. The videotapes of their conversations showed rather conspicuously that the members of the class exposed to body language training were much more inclined to communicate with appropriate proxemic, haptic, facial, and gestural modalities than those who were not.

Although the experiment did not constitute a scientific study in any sense of the term, it did point, obliquely at least, to the feasibility and practicability of incorporating body language instruction into SLT. Incidentally, it was also felt by the instructor of the experimental group that her students derived much more enjoyment from the whole learning experience than students normally did in her courses. She also suspected that the nonverbal training component helped to foster a positive attitude towards the other learning tasks in the course.

More than deriving practical pedagogical implications for teaching, a semiotic perspective of SLA has value in and of itself, because it emphasizes the fact that language is not an autonomous code, separate from the other codes humans employ to represent and communicate information, ideas, emotions, etc. The fact that semiotics has not yet worked its way into the everyday vocabulary of educational discourse, nor that of social discourse generally, bears witness to the fact that much remains to be done in raising awareness of its potential usefulness.

1.3.1 Semiotics

The principle that guides a semiotic investigation of SLA is that the process is a sign-based conceptual one. A *sign* is anything (a word, a gesture, a wink, a smile, etc.) that stands for something other than itself. A word such as *tree* does not stand for the sounds that comprise it, /tri/, but rather for something else—a type of plant that can easily be visualized and rendered pictorially. Similarly, a nonverbal sign, such as a finger pointing at something or someone, does not stand for itself, the finger; but rather for the someone or something to which it calls attention:

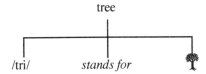

Figure 1. The sign *tree* and what it stands for

Modern-day theories of the sign trace their origins to the writings of the Swiss linguist Ferdinand de Saussure (1857-1913) and the American philosopher Charles S. Peirce (1839-1914). As an autonomous field of inquiry, semiotics has been expanded and developed throughout the twentieth century by such scholars as Charles Morris, Roland Barthes, Louis Hjelmslev, A. J. Greimas, Thomas A. Sebeok, and Umberto Eco, to mention but a few. There is no doubt that a large part of the recent increase in the popularity of semiotics has been brought about by the publication in 1983 of a best-selling medieval detective novel, *The Name of the Rose*, written by one of the most distinguished practitioners of semiotics today, Umberto Eco. Eco has since published other best-sellers—e.g. *Foucault's Pendulum* and *The Island of the Day Before*.

The ability to produce and understand signs is, as mentioned above (§1.2.1), called semiosis (Sebeok 1976, 1994). The etymology of this term is traceable to the Greek word *semeion* 'mark', 'sign'. In its oldest usage (Nöth 1990: 12-14), it referred to a specific kind of sign—a physiological symptom produced by a specific ailment or disease. It was used first by Hippocrates (460?-377? BC)—the founder of Western medical science—to alert medical practitioners to the value of knowing how to decipher the bodily signs that are both observable on their patients. The science of *semeiotika* was thus established so that medical practitioners could carry out accurate diagnoses of symptoms and formulate suitable prognoses. As the philosopher Max Fisch (1978: 41) points out, it was soon after Hippocrates' utilization of the term *semeion* to refer to a bodily symptom that it came to mean—by the time of Aristotle (384-322 BC)—the mental activity of using words, symbols, actions, etc. to stand for things in the world.

There are two main models of the sign used commonly today. Although some view them as antagonistic, a close analysis shows that they really are complementary in many ways. One model, as mentioned, is the Saussurean one. Saussure was born in Geneva in 1857. He attended science classes for a year at the University of Geneva before turning to language studies at the University of Leipzig in 1876. As a student he published his only book, *Mémoire sur le système primitif des voyelles dans les langues indo-européennes* (1879), an important work on the vowel system of Proto-Indo-European, considered the parent language from which the Indo-European languages descended. Saussure taught at the École des Hautes Études in Paris from 1881 to 1891 and then became a professor of Sanskrit and Comparative Grammar at the University of Geneva. Although he never wrote another book, his teaching proved highly influential. After his death, two of his students collated their lecture notes and other materials into the seminal work, *Cours de linguistique générale* (1916), that bears his name. It reveals Saussure's ground-breaking approach to language that became the basis for establishing both semiotics and linguistics as autonomous scientific disciplines in the twentieth century.

In the *Cours*, Saussure defined the sign as a mental entity made up of: (1) something physical—sounds, letters, gestures, etc.—which he termed the *signifier*, and (2) the *image* or *concept* that it evokes—which he called the *signified*. He dubbed the relation that holds between the two *signification*. Saussure considered the connection between the signifier and the signified an arbitrary one. To make his point, he remarked that there was no evident reason for using, say, *tree* or *arbre* (French) to designate an arboreal plant. Indeed, any well-formed signifier could have been used in either language—a well-formed signifier is one that is constructed in accordance with the orthographic or phonological rules of the language (*tree* is well-formed in English; *tbky* is not). Saussure did admit, however, that there were some instances whereby the signifier was fashioned in imitation of the signified. Onomatopoeic words (*drip*, *plop*, *whack*, etc.), he granted, were simulative of perceivable sounds. But Saussure maintained that this was a relatively isolated and infrequent occurrence in word-formation. Moreover, the highly variable nature of onomatopoeia across languages demonstrated to him that even this phenomenon was subject to arbitrary cultural judgments. For instance, the word used to refer to the sounds made by a rooster is *cock-a-doodle-do* in English, but *chicchirichí* (pronounced /kikkirikí/) in Italian; the word employed to refer to the barking of a dog is b*ow-wow* in English, but *ouaoua* (pronounced /wawa/) in French. Saussure suggested that such onomatopoeic creations were only approximate and more or less culture-specific imitations

Many semioticians have begged to differ with this specific part of Saussurean theory. What Saussure seems to have ignored is that even those who do not speak English, Italian, or French will notice an attempt in all the above signifiers to imitate rooster or canine sounds—an attempt constrained by the respective sound systems of the different languages that are, in part, responsible for the distinct phonic outcomes. Such attempts, in fact, probably went into the creation of most common words in a language, even though people no longer consciously experience them as physical simulations of their referents. This is because time and constant usage have made people forget the original onomatopoeic connection between signifier and signified.

Saussurean theory was developed and expanded throughout the twentieth century by the Danish linguist Louis Hjelmslev (1899-1965) and the French semioticians Roland Barthes (1915-1980) and Algirdas Julien Greimas (1917-1992), among others. Hjelmslev emphasized that signs encompass not only internal conceptual meaning—e.g. *tree* = 'an arboreal plant'—but a mass of information coming from outside the sign itself: namely, the historical meanings and connotations associated with the signified. Similarly, Barthes argued that a word like *lion* carries with it much more that a literal meaning, referring to the animal 'lion'. When it is used, it concomitantly implies qualities of 'fierceness', 'pride', etc. that are typically associated with *lions*.

Greimas expanded the idea of *opposition*, the view that two signs are kept recognizably distinct by the mental effect produced by a minimal difference between them. The words *pin* and *bin*, for instance, are recognizably distinct signs because the difference between their initial sounds /p/ and /b/ is sufficient to produce different signifieds: the former is a *voiceless* consonant (produced without the vibration of the vocal cords); the latter a corresponding *voiced* consonant (produced with the vibration of the vocal cords). Greimas claimed that binary semantic oppositions—e.g. *good-bad, tall-short, right-wrong*, etc.—were not enough to signal differences in meaning. So, he developed the concept of the *semiotic square*, by which the meaning of a word such as *rich* (s_1) can be gleaned when it is put in opposition simultaneously to its contradictory, *not rich* (-s_1), to its contrary, *poor* (s_2), and to its contradictory, *not poor* (-s_2):

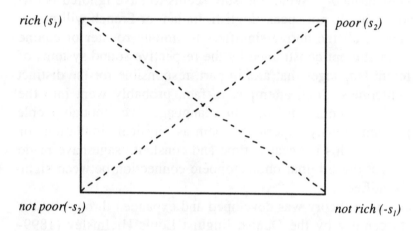

rich (s_1) .... *poor (s_2)*

not poor(-s_2) .... *not rich (-s_1)*

Figure 2. The semiotic square for *rich*

   The second main twentieth-century model of the sign comes, as mentioned, from the pen of Charles Peirce. Peirce was born in Cambridge, Massachusetts, in 1839. He was educated at Harvard University, and lectured on logic and philosophy at Johns Hopkins and Harvard universities. He conducted experiments to determine the density and shape of the earth and expanded the system of logic created by the British mathematician George Boole (1815-1864). But Peirce is best known for two things: (1) his philosophical system, later called *pragmatism*, which maintains that the significance of any theory or model lies in the practical effects of its application, and (2) for his model of the sign.

   Peirce called the physical part of the sign the *representamen*, defined as the physical strategy of representation itself (the use of sounds, hand movements, etc. for some representational purpose). He claimed that there were three kinds of *representamina* in human representational systems—*qualisigns, sinsigns,* and *legisigns.* A *qualisign* is a representamen that draws attention to, or singles out, some *quality* of its referent. In language, an adjective is a qualisign since it draws attention to the qualities (color, shape, size, etc.) of referents. In other codes, qualisigns include the colors used by painters and the harmonies and tones used by composers. A *sinsign* is a representamen that draws attention to, or singles out, a particular referent in time-space: e.g. a pointing finger, the words *here* and *there,* etc. A *legisign* is a representamen that designates something by convention: e.g. words referring to abstract concepts, symbols, etc.

Peirce termed the referent of the sign the *object*—a term taken from philosophy, meaning anything that could be known or perceived by the mind. Peirce observed that there were three kinds of *objects.* An object that has been represented through some form of replication, simulation, or resemblance is called an *iconically* represented object: e.g. a photo resembles its referent visually, a word such as *bang* resembles its referent phonically, and so on. A referent that has been represented through some form of indication is called an *indexically* represented object: e.g. a pointing index finger is an indication of where an object is in space, the word *here* similarly indicates where an object is; etc. A referent that has been represented conventionally is a *symbolic* object e.g. a *rose* is a symbol of love in some cultures, words such as *love* and *hope* refer by convention to various emotions or concepts, and so on.

Peirce described iconic representation as a *firstness* modality, because it is motivated by sensory perception. Iconic signs are physical substitutes for the referents themselves. Since they are fashioned in cultural contexts, Peirce used the term *hypoicon* to acknowledge this fact. A hypoicon can be figured out by those who are not necessarily a part of the culture, if told what the referent is. Peirce described indexes as *secondness* signs, because they refer to the existence and location of referents in time-space. Unlike icons, indexes are not substitutes for their referents. He defined symbols as *thirdness* forms of representation, because their meanings can be extracted only in terms of social convention

Finally, Peirce dubbed the meaning that one gets from, or intends with, a sign the *interpretant.* There were, in his view, three types of *interpretants:* (1) a *rheme,* which is the meaning that can be gleaned from a qualisign; (2) a *dicisign*, which is the meaning that can be extracted from a sinsign; and (3) an *argument*, which is how legisigns are understood. The first involves understanding qualities of things, the second the existence of things relative to one another other, and the third the arbitrary uses and functions of certain ideas and notions.

Peircean theory has received much attention on the part of twentieth-century semioticians. Among the most interesting expansions of Peircean theory is *modeling systems theory*, as developed by Thomas A. Sebeok (1920-) and members of the Tartu school of semiotics (e.g. Sebeok 1994). Sebeok argues that there are three types of modeling systems in the human species that make human representation highly advanced with respect to that of other species:

- the *Primary Modeling System* (PMS) = the neural system that predisposes the human infant to engage in simulative forms of semiosis, which in turn permit imitative and indicational representational activities;

- the *Secondary Modeling System* (SMS) = the more complex neural system that predisposes the human infant to engage in verbal forms of semiosis, which in turn permit linguistic representational activities;

- the *Tertiary Modeling System* (TMS) = the highly complex neural system that predisposes the maturing child to engage in highly abstract forms of semiosis which in turn permit symbolic representational activities (narration, art, etc.).

The PMS is essentially the system that undergirds iconicity in representation; the SMS indexicality and much of language; and the TMS advanced abstract language and symbolism. The usefulness of this theoretical framework is that it can be applied to investigate semiosis across species (Sebeok and Danesi 2000).

The basic perspective that undergirds all theoretical writing in semiotics is that the sign has a triadic nature. First, there is the physical sign itself, the sounds that comprise a word, the movements that define a gesture, the wave lengths that fix the limits of a color, etc.; this dimension of the sign, as we have seen, is called vicariously its *signifier, representamen,* or even just *sign.* Second, there is the sign's *referent,* also called its *object, concept, image,* or *signified*; this is the entity (object, event, idea, being, etc.) to which the sign refers and thus calls attention. Finally, there is the sign's *meaning,* known also as *signification* or as the *interpretant,* that results when the sign and the referent are linked together in a culturally-appropriate way. The *meaning* is not coincident with the *referent.* Even a concrete sign like the word *cat* can have various *meanings* that are shaped, on the one side, by previous experience with such mammals and, on the other side, by their cultural classification. Charles Morris (1938) added a fourth behavioral dimension to this basic model of the sign by emphasizing the physical as well as the purely cognitive responses that it elicits in the human being.

It is important to note from the outset that the term *sign* in language is not a simple synonym for *word.* A word, in fact, may be made up of one or several signifiers that convey "single pieces of meaning". For instance, the word *illogical* is segmentable into smaller units that also have meaning: (1) the basic form, *logic,* which has a lexical (dictionary) meaning, (2) the negative prefix *il-* which has a recurring functional meaning ('opposite of'), and (3) the suffix *-al* which also has a functional meaning ('the act or process of being something'). The study of how words are formed in a language, and what "bits and pieces"—known as *morphemes*—coalesce into the make-up and meaning of words, comes under the rubric of *morphology.* Morphemes may be: roots (as the *rasp-,* in *raspberry*), free lexical forms (*logic, play, boy*), endings (as the *-s* in *boys, -ed* in *played,* and *-ing* in *playing*), prefixes and suffixes (as the *il-* and *-al* in *illogical*), or internal alterations indicating grammatical distinctions (*sing-sang, mouse-mice,* etc.). The word *cats,* for instance, consists of two morphemes: *cat,* whose lexical meaning can be roughly rendered as 'feline animal', and *-s,* whose grammatical meaning is 'more than one'. *Antimicrobial,* meaning 'capable of destroying microorganisms', can be divided into three morphemes: *anti-* ('against'), *mi-*

crobe ('microorganism'), and *-ial* ('a suffix that makes the word an adjective').

Words can also be distinguished in terms of: (1) their dictionary meanings, in which case they are called *lexical items*; (2) the various phonic forms they manifest in the language, known as *syntactic forms*; or (3) how their forms are pronounced, known as *phonological forms*. Consider the word *learn*. First, note that it has a dictionary meaning, designating 'to gain knowledge or skill'. Second, note that forms such as *learned* and *learning* are not lexically-distinct words. Rather, they are different *syntactic forms* of the same lexical item. Third, note that the form *learned* can have two pronunciations: (1) when it is the verbal past tense it is pronounced as one syllable; (2) when it is used as an adjective (as in *the learned professor*), it is pronounced with two syllables.

1.3.2 Semiotic aspects of second language acquisition

Learning new words is not a simple matter of learning new morphemic patterns. It involves learning how the bits and pieces entail conceptual structures that may or may not exist in the NL. Consider, as a simple example, the difference between *orologio* in Italian and *watch* and *clock* in English. The Italian and English words refer to 'a mechanical device for registering the passage of time'. But in English the two words signal out for cognitive attention the 'portability' of the device—*watches* are worn or carried, *clocks* are put on tables, hung on walls, etc. No such attention is necessitated by the word *orologio*. Thus learning this new word entails some conceptual reorganization. The notion of 'portability' is not relevant in the use of *orologio*, but that of 'location' is (*table clock, wrist watch*, etc.). In Italian this is conveyed by *da* + locale: e.g. *orologio da tavolo* 'table clock', *orologio da polso* 'wrist watch', *orologio da muro* 'wall clock', etc.

As another example, consider English color terms. The light spectrum consists of a continuous gradation of hue from one end to the other. According to some physicists, there are potentially 8 million gradations that the human perceptual system is capable of distinguishing. If one were to put a finger at any point on the spectrum, there would be only a negligible difference in gradation in the colors immediately adjacent to the finger at either side. Yet, a speaker of English describing the spectrum will list the gradations as falling under categories such as *purple, blue, green, yellow, orange,* and *red.* This is because the speaker has been conditioned by English vocabulary to classify the content of the spectrum in specific ways. There is nothing inherently natural about the speaker's description; it is a reflex of English vocabulary, not of Nature.

By contrast, speakers of other languages are predisposed to describe the gradations on the very same spectrum in vastly different ways. Speakers of Shona, an indigenous African language, for instance, refer to the gradations with three terms, *cipswuka, citema,* and *cicena,* and speakers of Bassa, a language of Liberia, with two, *hui* and *ziza.* The specific color concepts one has acquired in cultural context in no way preclude the ability to perceive the color categories of other cultures. This is, indeed, what learners of another language end up doing when they study the new color terms: i.e. they learn how to reorganize the conceptual content of the spectrum in terms of new signifiers. Moreover, in all languages there exist signifiers for referring to more specific gradations on the spectrum if the situation should require it. In English the words *crimson, scarlet, vermilion,* for instance, make it possible to refer to gradations within the *red* conceptual range. But these are still felt by speakers to be *subcategories* of red, not distinct color categories on their own.

In 1969, the psycholinguists Berlin and Kay argued that differences in color terms are only superficial matters that conceal general underlying principles of color perception. Using the judgments of the native speakers of twenty widely-divergent languages, Berlin and Kay came to the conclusion that there were "focal points" in basic (single-term) color systems which clustered in certain predictable ways. They identified eleven universal focal points, which corresponded to the English words *red, pink, orange, yellow, brown, green, blue, purple, black, white,* and *gray.* Not all the languages they investigated had separate words for each of these colors, but there emerged a pattern that suggested to them the existence of a fixed way of encoding color across cultures. If a language had two colors, then the focal points were equivalents of English *black* and *white.* If it had three color terms, then the third one corresponded to *red.* A four-term system had either *yellow* or *green;* while a five-term system had both of these. A six-term system included *blue*; a seven-term system had *brown*. Finally, *purple, pink, orange,* and *gray* were found to occur in any combination in languages which had the previous focal points. Berlin and Kay found that languages with, say, a four-term system consisting of *black, white, red,* and *brown* did not exist.

The intriguing implications of this line of research were pursued vigorously in the 1970s by many psychologists. Eleanor Rosch (e.g. 1975a, 1975b), for instance, demonstrated that the Dani people of West Irian, who have a two-color system similar to the Bassa system described above, were able to discriminate easily eight focal points. Using a recognition-memory experiment, Rosch found that the Dani recognized focal colors better than non-focal ones. She also reported that they learned new colors more easily when the color names were paired with focal colors. Such findings suggested to Rosch that languages provided a guide to the interpretation of color, but they did not affect its perception in any way.

Semiotically speaking, color terms are verbal signifiers that encode specific signifieds. This entails that people are predisposed to attend primarily to the signifieds they have learned to discriminate through the color signifiers they know. This is a practical strategy; otherwise, millions of signifiers would need to be invented to classify the spectrum in terms of all the possible discriminations that can be made.

In addition to learning the literal meanings of color terms, students also face the task of learning the *connotations* associated with them. The topic of connotative conceptual structure will be discussed in chapter 4. Suffice it to say here that color terms are used not only to describe spectral phenomena *denotatively*, but also to convey moods, emotions, and social perspectives. This is why we say in English that people are *green with envy* or why we associate *redness* with a specific political ideology. As shall be discussed in subsequent chapters, such signifieds are hardly ornamental or inconsequential. The literal meanings of words and sentences make up a small portion of all potential meanings that signification produces. As anthropologist Roger Wescott (1980) has amply documented, color vocabularies seem to serve many more descriptive needs than just classifying hues.. In Hittite, for instance, words for colors initially designated plant and tree names such as *poplar, elm, cherry, oak,* etc.; in Hebrew, the name of the first man, *Adam,* meant 'red' and 'alive', and still today, in languages of the Slavic family *red* signifies 'living' and 'beautiful'.

1.4 Revisiting the SLT dilemma from a semiotic perspective

Throughout the twentieth century language educators searched constantly for ways to solve the SLT dilemma. They were guided in their search by the notions of linguistic and communicative competence, developing syllabi for each one. But as the proficiency movement has suggested, it is perhaps more appropriate, and certainly more useful, to think of the two kinds of syllabus as cooperative and complementary contributors to SLA in the classroom, not as antagonistic or mutually exclusive competitors. Even so, student discourse continues to manifest a conceptual unnaturalness that seems to be beyond such syllabi to counteract.

Simply out, student discourse is far too literal and devoid of target cultural meanings. What student discourse typically lacks, in other words, is what has been called above conceptual fluency. The reason for this, in my view, is that students have rarely studied the language in terms of how it reflects or encodes concepts on the basis of the culture's *signifying order.*

1.4.1 The signifying order

Culture is a system of shared and interconnected meanings that have been organized over time into *codes* (language, gesture, music, etc.). These make *signs* available for the construction of culturally-appropriate *texts* (conversations, narratives, musical compositions, etc.), and *figural assemblages* (metaphors, metonyms, etc.), through which concepts are communicated on a routine basis. This meaning-bearing system can be called a *signifying order:*

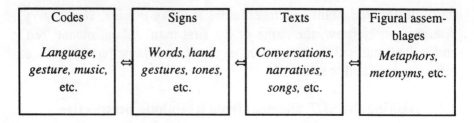

Figure 3. The signifying order

Signifying orders serve the function of making purposeful behavior, conceptual knowing, social interaction, and communication fluid and habitual. They are built from the same blueprint of structural properties that allow for the same patterns of representation and expression, as we shall see in the next chapter. These are manifest in the bodily schemas, language texts, myths, art works, rituals, performances, artifacts, and other signifying forms and expressions that constitute social life. The primary goal of semiotic analysis is to catalogue and analyze these manifestations in specific social situations.

As discussed above (§1.3.1), the sign encodes a referent in terms of three dimensions: (1) a physical dimension (sounds, hand movements, etc.) (= [A]); (2) a conceptual dimension (= [B]), which elicits a singular referent or a referential domain; (3) an interpretive dimension (= [A ⊃ B]). The formula [A ⊃ B] is used here to highlight the fact that the two parts of the sign are inextricably interlinked: i.e. the meaning of a sign is created the moment that a signifier is linked to a signified. Signifiers can, of course, exist without signifieds, as is evident in so-called "nonsense words"—i.e. well-formed words that do not have a meaning (*dop, flink, prip,* etc.). And, of course, there exists an infinitude of potential signifieds (referents or referential domains) that the current stock of signs in the world's languages have not yet encoded. Throughout the history of semiotics, there have been several attempts to identify and classify signs. Among these, Peirce's typology with 66 varieties, including intermediates and hybrids, is surely the most comprehensive, far-reaching, and sophisticated of all such attempts. In the verbal domain, one can also mention Roman Jakobson's (1970) classificatory system, which has shed considerable light on the minutiae of linguistic signification.

A *text* is a representation consisting of an arrangement of signi-fiers, but it is not conceptually equivalent to the aggregate of their signifieds. A novel, for instance, is made up of words following one after the other. But conceptually it is not just the sum of the mean-ings of the words; rather, a novel constitutes a *text* that generates its own signified(s). The meaning of a text is conditioned by *context*. The context is the situation—physical, psychological, and social—in which it is constructed, used, occurs, or to which it refers. Consider, for instance, the sentence *The pig is ready to eat.* The word *pig* in it has at least three meanings that are elicited by the separate social contexts in which the sentence is uttered:

- If uttered by a farmer during feeding time, the word *pig* will be understood in terms of its straightforward literal meaning, 'animal of the swine *(sus scrofa)* family'.

- If uttered by a cook who is announcing the fact that a pork meat dish is available for consumption, then the word *pig* will be understood as referring to something dif-ferent, 'meat from a pig'.

- If uttered critically by a person to describe someone with a ravenous appetite who is behaving gluttonously, then *pig* will be understood as referring to the negative char-acteristic displayed by the glutton.

A *code* in semiotic theory is defined simply as a system provid-ing particular types of signs that can be used in various ways and for diverse representational purposes. A language code, for instance, provides a set of signifiers that the producers and interpreters of words and verbal texts can recognize and convert into messages. Generally speaking, for some particular representational need there is an optimum code or set of codes that can be deployed. For example, the composer of a work of operatic art will need to deploy at least three codes in the construction of the operatic text—the musical code, the verbal code, and the theater code (all in place at the time of the composition).

Above all else a code allows human cultures to organize ideas, sensations, concepts, etc. in some systematic fashion. Organization provides for efficiency in retrieving information. An illustrative analogy may be useful at this point. A bibliophile may have, over the years, acquired thousands and thousands of books on every subject and by every author imaginable. Stockpiling them in a random fashion, however, will make it a time-consuming and inefficient chore for the bibliophile to locate a particular book. To make retrieval more efficient, the bibliophile will probably *organize* the books in various ways: e.g. putting them in alphabetical order according to author, arranging them in subject categories and then alphabetizing them according to author within each category, and so on. Each system of organization is a *code* that allows the bibliophile easy access to the location of some specific book.

A *figural assemblage* is a metaphor, metonym, or ironic construction that results through the assemblage of signifieds. The formula [thinking is seeing], for example, is a figural assemblage known as a conceptual metaphor because it delivers the abstract concept of [thinking] in terms of the signifieds associated with the concrete concept of [seeing]. In this book, such formulas will be included between square brackets. The [thinking is seeing] formula (which is largely unconscious in native speakers) underlies utterances such as the following:

1. Do you *see* what I am saying?
2. I can't quite *visualize* what happened.
3. Have you *looked at* that theory?
4. I *view* our relation differently from the way you do.
5. I can't quite *picture* that in my mind.
6. *Seeing* is believing, as they say.
7. I have no great *insight* into the matter.

Each of the two parts of the formula is called a *domain*: [thinking] is called the *target domain* because it is the abstract topic itself (the "target" of the assemblage); and [seeing] is called the *source domain* because it enfolds the concrete signifieds that deliver the meaning of the concept (Lakoff and Johnson 1980). A specific metaphorical statement uttered in a discourse situation is now construable as a particular externalization of such a mental formula. So, when we hear people using such statements as those cited above, it is obvious that they are not manifestations of isolated, self-contained metaphorical creations, but rather, specific instantiations of the [thinking is seeing] concept.

1.4.2 Conceptual reorganization

Research in semiotics has shown that concept-formation unfolds in terms of three types of signification—denotation, connotation, and metaphor. Referring to something denotatively, as we have seen, is not a simple matter of *one word-for-one meaning*. Recall the example of color terms above (§1.3.2). In order to learn the new denotative signifieds students will have to reorganize conceptually what they know about color classification in NL terms. Then, they will have to learn how the connotative and metaphorical meanings of the terms deliver signification in cultural (signifying order) terms. The primary task of learners can thus be seen to be one of *conceptual reorganization*: i.e. they will not have to learn the new color terms *tabula rasa*, but rather reorganize conceptually what they know already in new culturally-appropriate ways.

The notion of conceptual reorganization is not a theory of mind; it simply acknowledges that the SLA process inheres not in replacing one conceptual system with another, but in synchronizing the meanings of one to the other. The process is not predictable in terms of stages or of universal patterns—a viewpoint upon which virtually all psychological theories of SLA have been based. In actual fact, there are creative forces constantly at work in individual students. Constructs such as *stages*, *natural orders*, and the like are useful only to a certain extent. All that can be said with regard to the development of true conceptual fluency is that the teacher will have to have *patience* as each student goes through the learning process in an individualistic way. The goal of the teacher should be to allow the process to unfold unfettered by any rigid stage theory of SLA, or by any standardized SLT practices.

1.4.3 Interconnectedness

The notion of signifying order makes it explicit that there is an *interconnectedness* among the multifarious dimensions of representation and signification, from language to science and the arts. A digit in numerical representation, for instance, has the exact same structural features in semiotic terms that, say, a noun in language has—i.e. both are signs that derive their forms and meanings in terms of similar structural properties. The difference between a digit and a noun is thus not to be located in structural patterns, but in the different functions of the representational systems to which they pertain. This is why, despite their different cognitive functions, both are understandable in exactly the same way. In essence, the interconnectedness principle makes it obvious why such seemingly diverse forms of representation as poetry and mathematics are not mutually exclusive—with adequate exposure to both, people will be able to extract meaning from either one of them in remarkably similar ways.

Not only signs, but texts and codes are highly interconnected. A specific text bears meaning in a culture because it often alludes (in part or in whole) to already existing texts. For example, allusions to religious themes abound in novels, making their decipherment dependent upon knowledge of the culture's religious themes and images. Known as *intertextuality*, this manifestation of interconnectedness suggests that students reading SL narratives will hardly be able to grasp their cultural significance completely unless they are aware of the presence of other textual signifieds within it. The interconnectedness of codes can be called *intercodality*. Maps in Western culture are typically constructed with the principles of the code of Cartesian coordinate geometry, which was a separate code invented for a specific mathematical, not topographic, purpose (to unify algebra and geometry). The use of latitude and longitude lines to define locations on a map involves knowledge of this mathematical code, in which a point in the plane is defined in terms of coordinates which relate its location with respect to two perpendicular lines that intersect at an origin. So too, the use of gesture in communication along with verbal language entails an intercodal relation which, as we shall see in subsequent chapters, undergirds the delivery of oral speech. Meystell (1995) aptly portrays this interconnectedness as a *looping network*, whereby the various meanings loop around each other to produce the specific meanings required by the situation. As Meystell (1995: 112) cogently argues, this looping allows us to understand how all forms of knowledge, all forms of learning and thus, all the disciplines spring from the same source: "All the disciplines use the same way of thinking, they just use different symbols (terms) to explain it". It is his notion of *network* that will be developed in the next chapter and become the basis for the discussion of conceptual fluency to follow.

Chapter II
Conceptual structure

2. Introductory remarks

SLT has never before been so sophisticated as it is today. This is because, as we saw in the previous chapter, it has been shaped by theories and findings coming out of psychology and linguistics. This interplay between the research domain and instructional practices has produced teachers who are among the most informed and pedagogically-knowledgeable of all time.

So, why is there, despite the apparent sophistication, still so much discussion going on in scholarly journals, and among practitioners, about what to do to make student discourse more native-like? The recent literature has even rekindled an old debate: Should SLT continue to focus on developing in the learner a functional knowledge of the uses of the target language (communicative competence)? Or, should it return to the deployment of techniques and procedures whose aim is to foster in students control of grammar (linguistic competence)? This debate has been reignited, no doubt, because teachers continue to be frustrated by the inability of their students to speak in ways that go beyond the "textbook literalness" of classroom discourse. As discussed in the previous chapter, the most probable reason for this is the fact that students have had little opportunity, if any, to develop an overall *semiotic competence* in the SL—something decried only by a handful of educators (e.g. Lado 1957; Sebeok 1985). Semiotic competence can be defined, in essence, as the ability to interrelate the underlying structure of concepts to the surface grammar and vocabulary that reflects them

The purpose of this chapter is to present an overview of a descriptive apparatus—dubbed *network theory*—that has been designed specifically for the purpose of characterizing semiotic competence and of assessing its implications for SLT. Its main notions have been developed from several research projects conducted at both the University of Toronto and the University of Lugano during the academic years 1997-1998. Over 500 students were asked to draw up network analyses of over 200 common concepts, ranging from colors to emotions in English and Italian. Their analyses were then matched against the conceptual structures inherent in common written texts, such as newspaper and magazine articles in Toronto and Lugano. This revealed a high level of consistency between the student analyses and the actual manifestation of conceptual networks in written discourse, showing that native speakers can indeed access their unconscious knowledge of conceptual structure, if they are required to do so.

2.1 Concepts

In the 1980s the work on conceptual metaphors initiated by Lakoff and Johnson (e.g. Lakoff and Johnson 1980; Lakoff 1987; Johnson 1987), and a little later the research on the relation between concepts and grammar started by Langacker (1987, 1990), showed in tandem how verbal communication is shaped by a complex web of connotative and metaphorical meanings that are concealed in every word, phrase, and sentence. This line of inquiry, whether or not it is known or acknowledged by the scholars involved in it, is truly semiotic in its outlook. In a way, it has provided the theoretical coordinates for investigating semiotic competence in terms of its educational implications. Gearing SLT in all its components—methodology, materials development, testing, etc.—towards imparting conceptual fluency, without underplaying the roles of linguistic and communicative competence in SLA, entails teaching how the SL encodes concepts of all kinds (Danesi 1993a, 1993b; Russo 1997).

2.1.1 Network theory

In Saussurean semiotics, the term *concept* designates, basically, the conventional meaning we get from a sign. Concepts serve useful classificatory functions. Distinguishing, for instance, between *living* and *nonliving* things, between *people* and *animals*, between *males* and *females*, and so on constitute conceptual patterns that obviously serve various practical purposes for people cross-culturally. The psychologist Rosch (1973a) suggested that there were three such functions in semiotic systems:

- *superordinate*, which constitutes a highly general classificatory function—e.g. *feline, equine, human, animal*, etc.;

- *basic*, which is a typological function—e.g. *cat, tiger, lion*, etc. are types of *felines*;

- *subordinate*, which is a detail-providing function—e.g. *Siamese, tabby*, etc. are species of *cats*.

It is not a straightforward matter to explicate what a concept is by *using other words* to do so. Consider, for example, what happens when we look up the definition of a word such as *cat* in a dictionary. Typically, the latter defines a *cat* as 'a carnivorous mammal (*Felis catus*) domesticated since early times as a catcher of rats and mice and as a pet and existing in several distinctive breeds and varieties'. The problem with this definition is that it uses *mammal* to define *cat*. What is a *mammal*? The dictionary defines *mammal* as 'any of various warm-blooded vertebrate animals of the class Mammalia'. What is an *animal*? The dictionary goes on to define an *animal* as 'a living organism other than a plant or a bacterium'. What is an *organism*? An *organism*, the dictionary stipulates, is 'an individual animal or plant having diverse organs and parts that function together as a whole to maintain *life* and its activities'. But, then, what is *life*? *Life*, it specifies, is 'the property that distinguishes living organisms'. At that point it apparent that the dictionary has gone into a conceptual loop—it has employed an already-used concept, *organism*, to define *life*.

The concepts employed by the dictionary to define *cat* can thus be represented as follows:

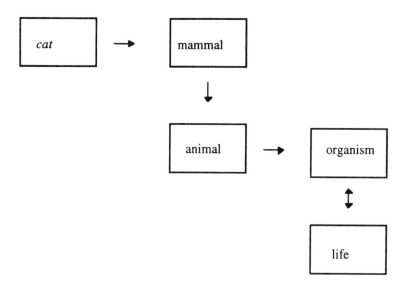

Figure 4. Conceptual loop created by a dictionary definition of *cat*

Looping is caused by the fact that definitions employ words, which of course encode other concepts, to define a concept. One way around this is to use imagery—e.g. a drawing or a photograph of a cat—as do so-called *visual dictionaries*. But this technique creates problems of a different nature (e.g. Which image or photo is the appropriate one culturally?). As it turns out, the dictionary approach described above is the appropriate one—for the reason that all human systems of knowledge have a looping associative structure, including mathematics, as the brilliant mathematician Kurt Gödel (1906-1978) demonstrated in 1931.

This suggests that the meaning of something can only be inferred by relating it to the meaning of something else to which it is associated. There simply is no such thing as an "absolute concept". So, the meaning of *cat* is something that can only be extrapolated from the circuitry of associations that it evokes. This circuitry can be called a *network*. In addition to the concepts of *mammal, animal, organism*, and *life*, used by the dictionary, one can add others such as *whiskers* and *tail* to the circuitry of the *cat* network:

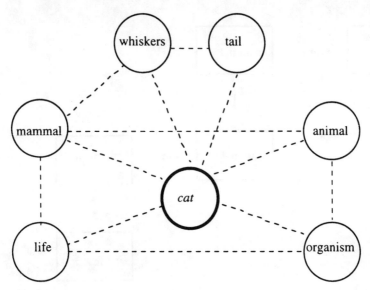

Figure 5. A conceptual network for *cat*

The above diagram is intended to show that the meaning of a concept such as *cat* crystallizes from an intricate interplay of associations that it evokes. Note the main characteristics about this network:

- the *mammal, animal, life*, and *organism* nodes in it form a primary circuit—circuits are groups of nodes connected by dotted lines;

- the *whisker* and *tail* nodes are generated by the *mammal* node, forming an "offshoot" secondary circuit;

- all the nodes are connected to *cat*—the conceptual focus of the network.

The nodes in a primary circuit will henceforward be called *primary nodes*, those in a secondary circuit will be called *secondary nodes*, those in a tertiary circuit will be called *tertiary nodes*, and so forth. There are several things about networks and network theory that must be made clear from the very outset:

- The term *theory* is not used in its strictly scientific sense, but rather in its original etymological sense of 'a view'. Network theory is not a "theory of concepts"—it is a descriptive apparatus for literally *viewing* on paper what dictionary makers have known for centuries—namely that the meaning of something is impossible to pin down without reference to other meanings.

- The position of nodes, the configuration of circuits, and the "distances" among nodes and circuits in a network reflect no necessary pattern or intrinsic structure: e.g. in the diagram above, the *mammal* node could have been located virtually anywhere vis-à-vis the other primary nodes to which it is interconnected. The only thing that is relevant about such diagrams is *how* the nodes are interrelated to each other.

- There is no limit (maximum or minimum) to the number and types of nodes and circuits that can be used to characterize a concept. It depends on a host of factors, not the least of which is the knowledge of the network-maker. In the above network, the secondary circuit generated by *mammal*, for example, could have been extended to contain *carnivorous, rodent-eater*, etc.; the *life* node could have been extended to generate a secondary circuit of its own containing nodes such as *animate, breath, existence*, etc. in no particular order; other nodes such as *feline, carnivorous, Siamese, tabby*, etc. could have been inserted to give a more detailed "picture" of the conceptual structure of *cat*; and so on.

- Network design will vary according to case and necessity. The above network has *cat* as its focal point because that is the concept under consideration. Such a node can be called a *focal node*. Focal nodes will be

identified, whenever necessary, with a thicker circum-
ference (as has been done above). However, if *animal*
were the focal concept, then *cat* would be represented
differently as a nonfocal node connected to it in a circuit that would also include *dog, horse*, among other
associated nodes. In effect, there is no way to predict
the configuration of a network in advance. It all depends on the analyst, on the purpose of the analysis,
on the type of concept, and on other such factors that
are variable and/or unpredictable.

The primary node concepts—*mammal, animal, life*, and *organism*—are superordinate ones; *cat* is a basic concept; and *whiskers* and
tail are subordinate concepts. Although it is beyond the purpose of
the present discussion, it would be interesting to investigate the relation of circuits (primary, secondary, etc.) to these functions and determine if a pattern emerges. That is something that will have to be
left for future work on network analysis. Clearly, the configuration of
a network will vary according to the function of its focal node—i.e. a
network that has a superordinate focal node (e.g. *mammal*) will dis-
play a different pattern of circuitry than will one that has a basic concept at its focal center.

2.1.2 Types of concepts

Semiotic research has identified three main types of concepts—
denotative, connotative, and metaphorical. These will be dealt with
respectively in the next three chapters. For the present purposes, it is
sufficient to point out that they are not to be considered separate conceptual phenomena, but rather, interconnected to each other through
various kinds of circuitry and network linkages.

Denotation is the initial meaning captured by a sign. The denotative meaning of the word *blue* in English, for instance, encodes the
image of a hue on the color spectrum with a wavelength of approximately 450 to 490 nanometers. The specific image that comes to
mind will be different from individual to individual. But all images
will fall within the above wavelength. The denotative concept of
"blueness" is forged by observing the hues found in natural phenom-

ena such as the sky and the sea, by observing other hues in things, and so on.

The denotative network for this focal node will thus contain circuits made up of nonfocal nodes such as *color, shade, hue, gradation, sky,* and *sea,* among others. Since *blue* is a type of color, it is really part of a conceptual, or network, domain that has *color* as its focal point. However, in specific network analyses, it is not necessary to show the relevant network domain—in which *blue* would, in effect, be configured as a primary node connected to *color.* A *network domain* can be defined as the associative configuration generated by superordinate categories—*color, animals,* etc. Within such domains, basic and subordinate concepts can be subdivided, for the purpose of a specific analysis, into smaller networks of their own. That applies to the network designed below, which nevertheless shows that *blue* is a type of color as is *yellow* and *green.* Note that specific network analyses need not provide great detail:

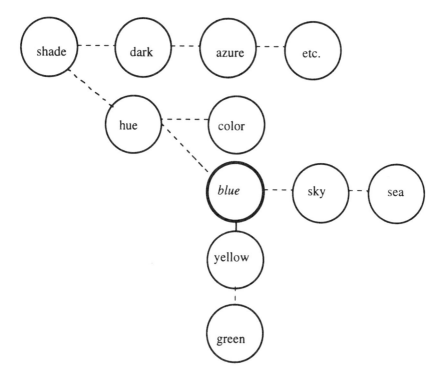

Figure 6. A denotative network for *blue*

Denotative networks allow speakers of a language to talk and think about concrete things in specific ways. But such networks are rather limited when it comes to serving the need of describing abstractions, emotions, morals, etc. For this reason they are extended considerably through further associative thinking. Consider the use of *cat* and *blue* in the following sentences:

8. He's a real cool *cat*.
9. Today I've got the *blues*.
10. She let the *cat* out of the bag.
11. That hit me right out of the *blue*.

These encode *connotative* and *metaphorical* meanings, which are "added" or "extended" meanings of the two signs. The use of *cat* in (8) to mean 'attractive', 'engaging', etc. comes out of the discourse associated with jazz music; and the use of *blues* in (9) to mean 'sad', 'gloomy', etc. comes out of the tradition of blues music talk. In effect, these have been added to the original networks of *cat* and *blue* through the channel of specific cultural traditions. They are nodes that interconnect *cat* and *blue* to the culture-specific conceptual nodes of *jazz* and *blues*:

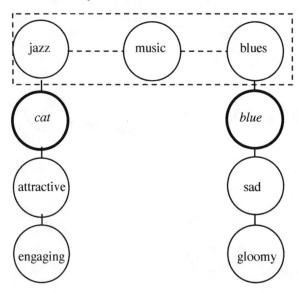

Figure 7. A connotative network for *cat* and *blue*

The use of a dotted rectangle in the above diagram is intended to show that *music* belongs to a different conceptual network, to which the *cat* and *blue* concepts have been associated by extension. This practice will be used from this point on. The meaning of 'something secret' associated with *cat* in (10) and the meaning of 'unexpectedness' associated with *blue* in (11) have resulted from associating *cats* with *secrecy* and *blue* with the color of the *sky*. Sentence (10) is, in effect, a specific instantiation of the conceptual metaphor [animals reflect human life and activities], which underlies common expressions such as:

12. It's a *dog's* life.
13. Your life is a *cat's* cradle.
14. I heard it from the *horse's* mouth.

Sentence (11) is an instantiation of the conceptual metaphor [Nature is a portent of destiny]—which literary critics classify as a stylistic technique under the rubric of *pathetic fallacy*. This underlies such common expressions as:

15. I heard it from an *angry wind*.
16. *Cruel clouds* are gathering over her life.

The networks that are generated by metaphorical signifieds will be discussed in detail in chapter 5. Suffice it to say here that these extend the meanings of signs within networks considerably. Comprehensive network analyses of *cat* and *blue* would have to show how all meanings—denotative, connotative, metaphorical—are interconnected to each other through complex circuitry. It is the ability to navigate through the overarching circuitry of such networks, choosing appropriate denotative, connotative, or metaphorical nodes according to need, and integrating them cohesively into appropriate individually-fashioned circuitry to match the need, that constitutes conceptual fluency in a language.

The connotative extensional process is, as mentioned, *associative*. But it is not one based on *association-by-sense*, as it is in the formation of denotative concepts. Rather, it is based on *association-by-inference*. To grasp what this means, consider the word *tail*, which the dictionary defines as 'the flexible appendage found at the rear end of an animal's body'. This is the denotative meaning of *tail* in utterances such as the following:

17. My cat's *tail* is over one foot long.
18. Are there any species of dogs without *tails*?
19. That horse's *tail* is rather short, isn't it?

In a denotative network *tail*—as a focal node would be connected to a circuit that contains *appendage* and *rear-end* nodes. These provide basic information about what a *tail* is—an extremity — and where it is found on an animal—on its rear end. Now, these nodes are what guide the extension of *tail* to encompass meanings such as following:

20. The *tail* of that shirt is not bleached.
21. Do you want heads or *tails* for this coin toss?
22. The *tail* section of that airplane is making a funny noise.

Such extensions are hardly random or disconnected to the original signified. Shirts, coins, and airplanes are inferred in English-speaking cultures as having appendages and rear ends. In network terms, a *shirt*, a *coin*, and an *airplane* are concepts that belong to separate networks of their own. However, through associative inference these are interlinked to the *tail* network. The process of network linking will henceforward be called *grafting*. Note the following things:

- Separate network domains are represented by dotted rectangles.

- Linkages among networks often show nodes criss-crossing.

- *Crisscrossing* is, in fact, a salient visual characteristic of grafting.

- In such analyses, too, only the relevant details will be shown. It is not necessary to provide complete circuitry and linkages for the purpose of specific analyses:

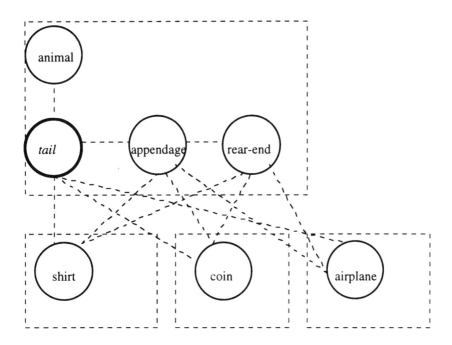

Figure 8. Connotation produced by grafting

Connotation is the operative mode in the production and decipherment of creative texts such as poems, novels, etc.—in effect, of most non-mathematical and non-scientific texts. The latter, on the other hand, are constructed and interpreted primarily in denotative ways. But this does not mean that meaning in science is encoded only denotatively. On the contrary, many of the theories and models of science, as the philosopher Max Black (1962) among others have shown, are born of associative metaphorical thinking, even though they end up being used and interpreted denotatively over time. The theory of atomic structure, for instance, is presented as a tiny universe, with a sun (nucleus) and orbiting planets (electrons, protons, etc.). The end result is a theory that extends a model that at the time it was fashioned was already familiar to scientists.

Network theory makes it obvious that many, if not most, of the customs, rituals, and practices of a culture are interconnected meaningfully through associative thinking. As a practical example, consider the phenomenon of *naming*. A *name* identifies a person in relation to other persons. But the name-giving process is hardly a random one. Even in the West, where name-giving is a relatively open and unregulated process, it is nonetheless shaped by specific customs and trends. The sources of first names, for instance, include: (1) Judeo-Christian tradition (*Sarah, David, Rebecca, Luke*, etc.), (2) the domain of Nature (*Brook, Daisy, Margaret*, etc.), (3) the classical domain (*Alexander Diana, Helen, Jason*, etc.), (4) the calendar (*June, Domenic*, etc.), (5) pop culture (*Ringo, Neve*, etc.), (6) characterization (*Happy, Serene, Joy, Clare*, etc.). Surnames are, of course, passed on through the kinship line. However, originally, they were assigned on the basis of place (*Appleby*), descendancy (*Johnson*), occupation (*Smith*), or some identifying physical or social feature (*Faithful*). In effect, names are interlinked to circuits in separate network domains, allowing people to extract historically-based and socially-relevant meanings from them.

As we shall see in chapter 5, network-grafting is primarily metaphorical in etiology. Consider, as an example, the statement *The professor is a snake*. The parts of the metaphor are named as follows:

- the primary referent, *professor*, is called the *topic*;

- the secondary referent, *snake*, is called the *vehicle*;

- their assemblage is called the *ground*.

Metaphor creates a new meaning through a double process of transferal and interaction: i.e. the meaning of the vehicle, *snake*, is transferred to the topic, *professor*, where it interacts conceptually with it. Now, it is not the denotative meaning of the vehicle, *snake*, that is transferred to the topic, but rather its connotative meanings, namely the culture-specific characteristics perceived in snakes— 'slyness', 'danger', 'slipperiness', etc. It is this circuit of connotations linked to *snake* that are grafted onto the *professor*. The network domain to which *snake* belongs is, as we saw in the previous chapter (§1.4.1), called the *source domain*; the domain to which *professor* belongs is called the *target domain*. The grafting of the connotative nodes associated with the source domain circuit onto the focal target domain node is what creates the meaning (or ground) of the metaphor:

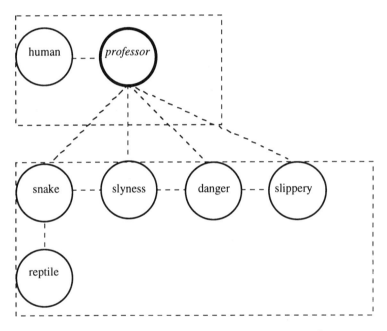

Figure 9. Grafting the domain of *snake* onto the domain of *professor*

The linguist George Lakoff and the philosopher Mark Johnson showed in 1980 how metaphorical concepts are forged systematically and how they cluster into general concepts. The above expression— *The professor is a snake*—is hardly an isolated example of metaphorical fancy; rather, it is one of many similar expressions that cluster around the idea that [human personality] is understandable in terms of [animal features]:

23. John is a *pig*.
24. That woman is a *bear*.
25. My friend is a *gorilla*.
26. Your dad is a *mouse*.
27. Don't try to *weasel* your way out of this.
28. You keep *hounding* me for nothing.
29. There is a *mole* in this organization.
30. He's a real *tiger*, isn't he?
31. She *roars* when she gets angry.
32. Are you trying to *snake* your way around the issue?

Each of the above is a specific instantiation of that very idea—namely [human personality is understandable in terms of animal features], or simply [people are animals]. This is dubbed a *conceptual metaphor* by Lakoff and Johnson. Note that the grafting of vehicular meanings in the metaphorization process is not based on linking denotative circuits, but connotative ones. Thus, it is not the reptilian physical qualities of snakes, or the feline qualities of tigers, that are connected to [people], but rather the kinds of behavioral characteristics that snakes and tigers are thought to have in human terms. This is what creates the interaction in metaphor. It is not a simple transferal process, but one based on *association-by-inference*, as it has been called above. Using electric current as an analogy, it can be said that such circuits run on "alternating current", so to speak.

Specifically, a conceptual metaphor is created by the grafting of the source network domain of *animals* onto the target network domain of *people* to produce a new linkage among disparate network domains. Note the following things:

- Again it is not necessary in such network analysis to provide detail, such as showing all the relevant criss-crossing circuits.

- Moreover, it is not necessary to show how the vehicle is converted into a noun, adjective, verb, etc. That is a surface structure process, as we will see below—e.g. if *snake* is the vehicle, then it can surface in speech as the noun *snake*, but also as the verb *slide,* the adjective *slippery,* etc., as the case may be.

- These are, of course, connotative nodes associated with *snake* its the source domain:

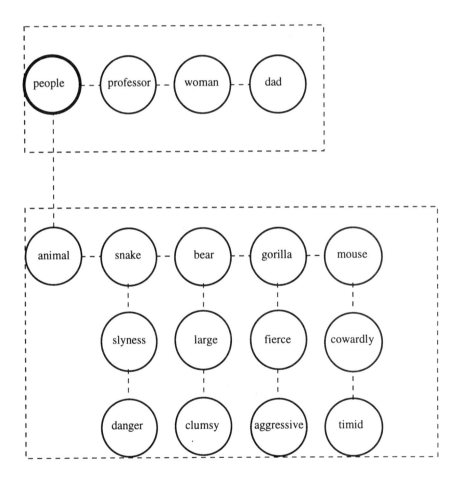

Figure 10. Conceptual metaphor grafting

2.2 Surface structure

Associative conceptual structure is convertible into linear surface structure through a process that henceforward will be called *re-flexivization*. Consider, for example, an underlying circuit containing *snake* as a metaphorical concept that is to be used in a specific speech act. In the surface language that is chosen to deliver it, it can show up as a verb (32), if it is the snake's movements that are grafted onto the target, or as an adjective (33), if it is a serpentine quality that is grafted conceptually onto the target:

33. The professor *snaked* his way around the issue.
34. The professor has a *snaky* way of doing things.

The difference between the two surface forms—*snaked* and *snaky*—can be traced to underlying circuits that extend the *snake* concept in specific ways. In (32) the nodes *move* and *before* (which indicates that the moving occurred in the past) are the relevant ones:

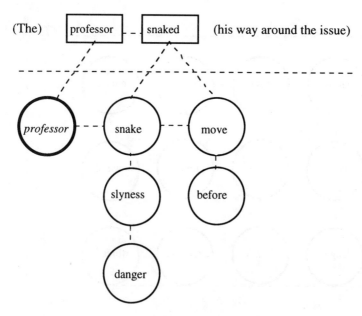

Figure 11. Reflexivization of *the professor snaked*

Note that the surface level is shown above the horizontal dotted line with the conceptual level below it. This convention will be used henceforward. Note as well that it is not necessary to show detailed circuitry in such diagrams. It is necessary to show only the relevant components involved in reflexivization. Finally, note that surface structure forms are enclosed in rectangles, so as to differentiate them from conceptual forms. This practice will also be adopted from this point on.

The reflexivization of (33) can be shown as follows. In this case the relevant node added to the underlying conceptual circuitry is *quality*:

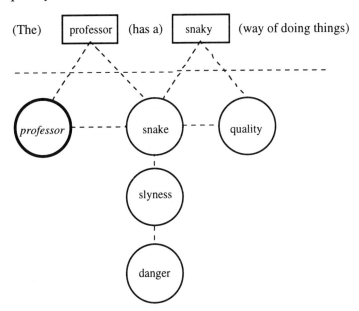

Figure 12. Reflexivization of *the professor has a snaky way*

The notion of reflexivization is not a theory of grammar. It is a heuristic technique for showing on paper how words, phrases, and sentences may be purported to reflect conceptual structure. Needless to say, surface structure reflects not only concepts, but is also sensitive to communicative functions, situational variables, stylistic needs, etc. This aspect of surface structure will not be dealt with in this book. The focus here is specifically on the reflexivization of conceptual structure.

Much work has already been done on the surface-communication interface (e.g. Halliday 1973, 1975; Tannen 1989).

There are literally an infinitude of ways in which the reflexivization of concepts can unfold. The choices made by the speaker, the context of the speech act, the grammatical and lexical knowledge of the speaker, etc. are the factors that constrain surface structure outcomes. It is not the purpose of reflexivization analysis to consider these factors. The main objective of such analysis is showing how grammar, vocabulary, and concepts are interconnected in a general way.

2.2.1 Surface codes

Reflexivization entails knowledge of the *surface codes*—grammar and vocabulary—that make the expression of concepts a physical reality. These provide the specific signs and their rules of arrangement for delivering concepts in a physical linear form. The focus of the structural syllabi in SLT was on imparting knowledge of such codes, independently of how they made the expression of concepts possible. It is not the purpose to describe them in any detail in this book. The relevant literature on surface-code learning is rather extensive and need not be revisited here. The bibliography at the back of this book contains various references to this literature.

There are three main structural relations that characterize these codes that are nevertheless worthwhile describing briefly. They are known generally in semiotics as *paradigmaticity, syntagmaticity*, and *substitution*.

Paradigmaticity is the relation that keeps signs recognizably different. Consider the following pairs of words in English:

35. pin *vs.* bin
36. fun *vs.* pun
37. duck *vs.* luck
38. cat *vs.* bat

What allows us to detect a difference in their meaning are the minimal phonic differences between initial /p/ and /b/ (35), /f/ and /p/

(36), /d/ and /l/ (37), and /k/ and /b/ (38). Needless to say, paradig-maticity is a feature of all codes. In music, for instance, a major and minor chord of the same key are perceivable as distinct on account of a half tone difference in the middle note of the chord; the left and right shoes of a pair of shoes are identifiable in terms of the orienta-tion of the shoe; and so on. Again, the nature of the learning task that paradigmaticity entails in the SL will not be of concern here, for it has been examined thoroughly by the relevant literature.

Now, note that the words in examples (35)-(38) above are not only differentiable relative to each other, but they are also recogniz-able as English words because their constituent sounds have been combined in ways that are consistent with English syllable structure. On the other hand, *tpin, tbin, tfun, tpun, tduck, tluck, tcat, tbat* would not be recognized as legitimate words in English because they would violate its syllable structure. Syllable structure is known technically as *syntagmatic* structure. Syntagmaticity is a combinatory property of surface forms. It is, of course, characteristic of all codes. In music, for instance, a melody is recognizable as such only if the notes fol-low each other in a certain way (e.g. according to the rules of har-monic progression); two shoes are considered to form a pair if they are of the same size, style, and color; and so on.

Substitution is an equivalence relation, by which one type of sign can be replaced by another in certain specific situations or for particular purposes. The English word *cat* is replaceable with the Spanish word *gato* for purposes of translation if a denotative mean-ing is required; words such as *thus, therefore,* and *consequently* can replace each other in texts for the purpose of avoiding repetition; and so on. This relation too characterizes all codes—European playing cards can replace American cards if an analogy is made between European and American suits; Roman numerals can replace Arabic numerals through simple conversion; and so on.

2.2.2 Reflexivization

Reflexivization can unfold in a variety of ways. In the formation of many words, for instance, it manifests itself as an *iconic* process (chapter 1, §1.3.1). Onomatopoeic words, for example, are iconic signs that attempt to replicate the sounds that certain things, actions, or movements are perceived to make:

39. It made a *zapping* sound.
40. I heard a *boom* behind the wall.
41. My bones were *scrunched* by that collision.
42. I heard a *smack* over there.

In example (39), the word *boom* contains two phonemes, /b/ and /m/, which, by their physical nature, can relay a certain type of deep, resonant sound that something is perceived to make, such as, for instance, an explosion. The word *boom*, in other words, reflects a sound property associated with certain concepts:

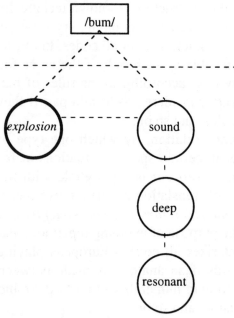

Figure 13. Iconic reflexivization

The linguist Morris Swadesh (1971) drew attention to such inbuilt iconic features in many of the world's tongues as the presence of [i]-type vowels to express "nearness"—as in English *here* and *near*—in contrast to [a]- [o]- and [u]-type vowels to express the opposite notion of "distance"—as in English *far* and *there*. The concept of *nearness* tends to surface tends to be reflected by the relative nearness of the lips in the articulation of [i] and other front vowels, and the complementary concept of *distance* by the relative openness of the lips in the pronunciation of [a], [æ], [u] and other mid and back vowels.

Iconicity in language manifests itself in a variety of surface forms. Here are just a few of them:

- repeating sounds in order to relay various effects— *sing-song*; *no-no*, etc. (alliteration)

- lengthening sounds so as to convey emphasis through them—*Yesssss!, Noooooo!*, etc.;

- using intonation to encode emotional states, to emphasize, to shock, etc.—*Are you absolutely sure? Noooooo way!*;

- making up words to reflect sound effects—*Zap!, Pow!*, etc.;

- employing certain phonemes or phonic clusters to encode the sound properties of referents—e.g. describing a snake as *slithery, slippery, sneaky*, etc.;

- increasing the loudness of the voice so as to convey a state of anger; whispering to convey secrecy, conspiracy, etc.

- increasing the rate of speech to convey urgency.

Differences in surface linear order are often due to underlying conceptual dichotomies. In Italian, for instance, the difference between the denotative and connotative meaning of an adjectival concept is sometimes reflected in the surface by a difference in position with respect to the noun:

After (denotative meaning)

43. *Lui è un ragazzo grande* ('He's a big boy').
44. *Lui è un uomo povero* ('He's an indigent man').

Before (connotative meaning)

45. *Lui è un grande amico* ('He's a great friend').
46. *Lui è un povero uomo* ('He's a miserable, forlorn man').

The different reflexivization processes pertaining to *povero* can be shown as follows:

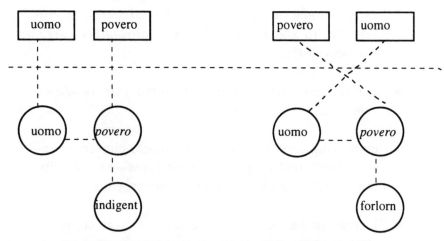

Figure 14. Reflexivization of a denotative-connotative adjectival dichotomy

Langacker (e.g. 1987, 1990) has argued that some nouns encode the conceptual difference *bounded* and *unbounded*—e.g. a count noun encodes a concept referring to something with boundaries; whereas a mass noun encodes a concept referring to something without them. Thus, for example, the noun *leaf* in English refers to something that has a boundary; whereas, a noun like *water* refers to something that does not. This conceptual dichotomy has consequences on the surface grammar: *leaves* can be counted, *water* cannot, thus *leaf* has a plural form, *water* does not (unless the referential

domain is metaphorical); *leaf* can be preceded by an indefinite article
(a leaf), *water* cannot; and so on. Similar structural effects are observable in other representational systems—in painting, for instance,
water is represented either with no boundaries or else as bounded by
other figures (land masses, the horizon, etc.); *leaves,* on the other
hand, can be depicted as separate figures with defined boundaries.

Verbs encode conceptual nodes such as *now*, *before*, and *after*.
These are reflected in surface morphemic structure that relays time
differences (known as *tense*). The difference between, say, *I am eating* and *I ate* is a reflex of the conceptual dichotomy *now* and *before*:

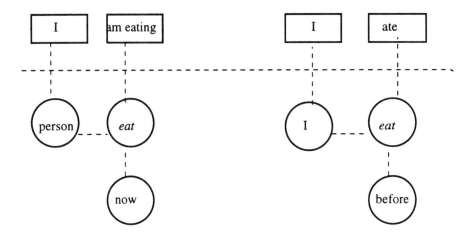

Figure 15. Reflexivization of an indexical dichotomy

Tense dichotomies are indexical in nature. An *index* is a sign
that refers to something or someone in terms of its existence or location in time, space, or in relation to something or someone else. Indexes are designed to indicate or show where they are in relation to
each other. The most typical manifestation of indexicality is the
pointing *index* finger, which humans the world over use instinctively
to point out and locate things, people, and events in the world. Verb
tense is a manifestation of temporal indexicality.

Indexicality is not only an intrinsic feature of concrete verbal
concepts, but also, by connotative and metaphorical extension, of

abstract ones. Take, for example, the following English sentences (Danesi and Santeramo 1995; Fillmore 1997):

47. When did you *think up* that preposterous idea?
48. You should *think over* carefully what you have just said.
49. *Think out* the entire problem, before coming to a solution.
50. I cannot *think straight* today.
51. Go ahead and *think* that problem *through*.

These expressions are the result of network grafting—i.e. of the grafting of the conceptual metaphor domain [ideas are objects] onto the domain of indexical concepts such as *up*, *over*, etc. The verb form *think up* elicits a mental image of upward movement, thus portraying an *idea* as an object seen to be extracted physically from a kind of mental terrain; *think over* evokes the image of scanning *ideas* with the mind's eye; *think out* elicits an image of extracting an *idea* so that it can be held up to the scrutiny of the mind's eye; *think straight* produces an image of sequential, and thus logical, movement of an *idea* from one point to another via a straight linear path; and *think through* generates an image of continuous, unbroken movement through space. This abstract form of metaphorical indexicality thus allows speakers to locate and identify abstract ideas in relation to spatiotemporal contexts, although such contexts are purely imaginary. It transforms the physiology of vision into a "physiology of thinking".

In sum, it must be emphasized again that the notion of reflexivization is not a theory of grammar. It is proposed simply to show that in the same way that a painting is much more than an assemblage of lines, shapes, colors, and melodies a combination of notes and harmonies, so too a sentence in language is much more than an assemblage of words and phrases built from some rule system in the brain. We use the surface grammatical and lexical codes at our disposal to model the world of concepts in ways that parallel how musicians use melodic elements and painters visual one to model it.

2.3 Pedagogical considerations

The most obvious implication that is inferable from the foregoing discussion is that the development of semiotic competence in the SL entails knowing how target language concepts are converted into surface structure grammar and vocabulary. More specifically, it entails knowing:

- how denotative, connotative, and metaphorical concepts are interconnected to each other and to the signifying order via associative networks (conceptual fluency);

- how to convert conceptual structures into surface structures (reflexivization).

- what grammatical and lexical resources are available to do so.

The development of these kinds of knowledge and abilities cannot be divided into a *natural order*, nor can they be guaranteed to emerge from simple exposure to input structured according to some stage model of SLA. Associative thinking processes require a considerable amount of time to develop in the SL.

The second main implication is that intensive practice of surface structure—*langue*—and of communicative routines—*parole*—is not sufficient to produce conceptual fluency as a byproduct. The *langue-parole* dichotomy was introduced into linguistics by Saussure (1916), who used the analogy of a chess game to illustrate what this entails. To engage in a game of chess both players must first know the *langue* of chess—the rules of movement and the overall strategy of how to play. This part of the game is "mind work". *Langue* imposes constraints on, and provides a guide to, the choices each player can make in the act of playing the game. The choices characterize *parole*—the ability to apply the abstract knowledge of chess *(langue)* to a specific game-playing situation.

Structural syllabi in SLT were organized around *langue*. The goal of instruction was, in effect, to impart control of surface structure. The development of *parole* was assigned a secondary status and thought to emerge gradually, on its own, from reading target language texts, from hearing taped conversations, and from various other modes of exposure to SL texts. The idea that *langue* and *parole* were two sides of the same coin was introduced into general linguistics and into the mindset of SL teachers by Hymes' notion of *communicative competence* (chapter 1, §1.1.5). Hymes claimed, in essence, that the forms of language were sensitive to the requirements of the communicative situation. Methods and approaches guided by this notion focused primarily on imparting *parole*. Communicative syllabi were organized to follow a sequence of increasing communicative complexity. Situational practice constituted the main pedagogical technique. The reading of authentic texts, the use of taped conversations, and the use of played a much larger role than they did in structuralist methods. Grammar (verb tenses, cases, etc.) was introduced in terms of the relevant communicative notions.

To grasp the main difference between a structuralist and communicative approaches, consider the treatment that the partitive structure in Italian would receive by each one The partitive is composed of the preposition *di* and the various forms of the definite article which are inflected according to the gender, number, and initial sound of the following noun (or adjective):

52. *dei libri* ('some books')
53. *delle matite* ('some pencils')
54. *degli studenti* ('some students')
55. *della carne* ('some meat')

In a structural syllabus this structure would be introduced only *after* the prepositions, articles, and rules of contraction had been learned and reinforced:

56. *di + i = dei*
57. *di + le = delle*
58. *di + gli = degli*

59. *di + la = della*
    etc.

In a communicative syllabus, on the other hand, the partitive would be introduced whenever it was required in the given sequence of functions to carry out some communicative task. Its surface structure features would be discussed at that point, whether or not students had been exposed to prepositions, articles, and/or rules of contraction:

Function: ordering food and beverages

60. *Io prendo della carne* ('I'll take some meat').
61. *Vorrei del caffè* ('I would like some coffee').
    etc.

Function: buying things

62. *Maria vuole comprare delle matite* ('Mary wants to buy some pencils').
63. *Vogli dei libri* ('I want some books').
    etc.

Students taught by either approach, however, continue to experience considerable difficulty in knowing when and how to use the partitive (Danesi and Di Pietro 1991). The most likely reason for this is that they have not been taught to perceive a relationship between the concept of *partiality* and the surface structure forms that deliver it. In a phrase, they have not been taught to think of the partitive as part of the signified of nouns. They have been taught either to control its surface form (in structuralist approaches) or else to use it in specific situations (in communicative approaches). In a semiotic approach the focus of instruction would be precisely on the signified (conceptual) component of nouns. This means instilling into students the ability to answer the following two relevant conceptual questions: (1) In what network domains does the concept of *partiality* occur? (2) How is it reflexivized according to domain? With respect to the second question, note that in Italian only singular forms of the partitive are used with mass nouns, and only plural ones with count nouns. This entails a reflexivization process that is tied to the *bounded* and *unbounded* dichotomy associated with nouns (see above §2.2.2):

With mass nouns

64. *Voglio della carne* ('I want some meat').
65. *Prendo del vino* ('I'll take some wine').
    etc.

With count nouns

66. *Ho comprato dei libri* ('I bought some books')
67. *Hanno comprato delle matite* ('They bought some pencils').
    etc.

The central task facing students in SLA is, clearly, that of conceptual reorganization (chapter 1, §1.4.2). Learning a new word, a new expression, or a new point of grammar implies, *unavoidably*, learning a new way of conceptualizing something. To grasp what this means, consider how native speakers of English would respond to the question *What is love?* posed by a four-year-old child. Clearly, they would not respond with a denotative dictionary definition of love as a *strong affective feeling towards someone*. What they are more likely to do is to relate the "experience" of love to something that is familiar to children—e.g. *Love is the feeling you get when your mummy or daddy kisses you*. Or else they might tell the child a story that illustrates what love is all about. The examples and stories we tell children are built from knowledge of the various conceptual networks that are available to us as native speakers of a language.

Since concepts are formed through association, it follows that teaching conceptual fluency will have to focus on providing conditions and occasions for associative thinking to occur. Consider, for instance, the task of learning a color concept. The task facing English-speaking students of Italian is that they will have to learn to refer to "blueness" in a different manner—in Italian the word *blue* is rendered by three terms—*celeste* ('light blue'), *azzurro* ('medium blue'), *blu* ('dark blue'). In the English network for *color, blue* is a basic concept and thus a primary node; *light* and *dark* are secondary nodes (subordinate concepts) associated with it. In the corresponding Italian network *celeste, azzurro,* and *blu* are primary nodes (basic concepts) connected to *colore* ('color'), which in turn have their own shade nodes *chiaro* 'light' *scuro* 'dark' , etc.

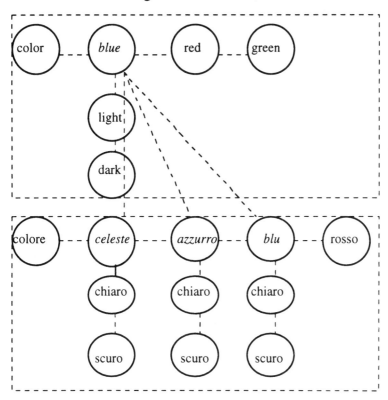

Figure 16. Comparing conceptual networks for "blueness"

Students will thus have to learn to associate new words with new meanings as shown in the diagram above. This is especially true in the extended network for *blue* that includes connotative nodes. There is no exact counterpart for *out of the blue* in Italian. The closest expression conceptually in that language is *cadere dalle nuvole* 'to fall from the clouds' which, of course, is formed in another network. When students attempt to express themselves with this concept, they typically produce a meaningless expression such as *L'ho sentito fuori dall'azzurro* (an asterisk is used to indicate an anomalous form), which is a word-by-word rendering of *I heard it out of the blue*. Such anomalous forms are recognizable, on the surface level, as consisting of Italian words. But they understandable only in English conceptual terms. They are, in a phrase, Italian forms with English meanings.

Take, as another example, the task of learning so-called deceptive cognates, known figuratively as *false friends*. These are words that derive from the same etymological source but have developed different meanings. In Italian, the word *sensibile* is not equivalent in meaning to the English cognate *sensible* ('rational'); in Italian it means 'sensitive'. Initially, students assume that the signifieds are identical, because of the surface similarity of the signifiers. In English *sensitive* and *rational* belong to different networks. The learning task can be shown as one consisting in associating *sensibile* with the appropriate network as follows—a process that can be called *network alignment*:

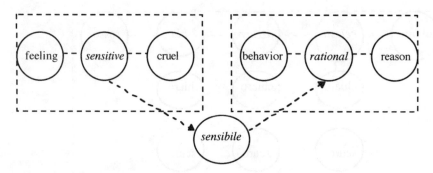

Figure 17. Network alignment

Such alignments will have to take place in all areas of SLA. This is particularly true with respect to the connotative networks that certain concepts entail. Consider, for instance, the concept of *health*. What is considered to be healthy in one culture may not coincide with views of health in another. Health cannot be defined ahistorically, aculturally or in purely absolutist terms. This does not deny the existence of events and states in the body that will lead to disease or illness. All organisms have a species-specific bodily warning system that alerts them to dangerous changes in bodily states. But in the human species bodily states are also representable and thus interpretable in culture-specific ways. This is why in some cultures a "healthy body" is considered to be one that is lean and muscular. Conversely, in others it is one that we in the West would consider too plump and rotund—although this was not the case not too long ago. A "healthy lifestyle" might be seen by some cultures to inhere in rigorous physical activity, while in others it might be envisaged as inhering in a more leisurely and sedentary form of behavior.

These *concepts* of health are dispersed throughout the signifying order. This implies that the meanings captured within one code are found in different surface form in other codes as well. So, the images of a healthy body that one finds in nonverbal codes (in media images, fashion trends, dieting vogues, etc.) will also be found in the verbal code. This is why we say such things as the following in English:

68. I'm too fat and out of shape.
69. My body is lean and in perfect working order.
70. To look better I have to lose weight.
71. I'm going to work out to improve my image.

Such expressions would have no meaning in a culture where a different conceptualization of health has been encoded. Not only body image, but even diseases are interconnected with other meaning systems of the signifying order through connotation and metaphorization. As the writer Susan Sontag wrote in her compelling 1978 book, *Illness as Metaphor*, although illness is not a metaphor, the signifying order invariably predisposes one to think of specific illnesses in certain ways. Using the example of cancer, Sontag (1978: 7) pointed out that in the not-too-distant past the very word *cancer* was said to have killed some patients who would not have necessarily succumbed to the malignancy from which they suffered: "As long as a particular disease is treated as an evil, invincible predator, not just a disease, most people with cancer will indeed be demoralized by learning what disease they have". Sontag's point that people suffer more from thinking about their disease than from the disease it-self is, indeed, a well-taken and instructive one.

Clearly, English-speaking SL learners of, say, Punjabi, Farsi, Cantonese, or any non-European language will have to adapt their understanding of health with how it is conceptualized in the target culture. The primary task facing SL learners is, clearly, a *reorganizational* one. Such reorganization can be *isomorphic*, whereby the surface forms of the NL and the SL reflect virtually the same conceptual structures, *overlapping*, by which they have overlapping circuitry, and *differentiated*, whereby they have completely different network structure. A case of isomorphism can be seen, for example, between the word *car* in English and *automobile* in Italian—leaving out differences that occur at the level of the interpretant, since an Italian *automobile* evokes different perceptions than does an American *car.* Isomorphism is, in any case, rare. Even among phylogenetically-related languages (e.g. English and German), it is exceptional to find signifiers covering the same stretches of meanings exactly. More than likely, there will be some overlap between the conceptual domains mapped by signifiers, as we have seen above with regard to color terms. A case of differentiation is the one mentioned above between English *sensible* and Italian *sensibile.*

The second task facing learners is how to reflexivize the new concepts in grammatically and lexically appropriate ways. As we saw above (§2.2.2) in Italian the position of certain adjectives vis-à-vis nouns will vary according to the denotative or connotative meaning intended. This is not the case in English. Reflexivization implies teaching the forms and rules of the surface codes in a way that allows students to see how they relate to the concepts they encode. Various pedagogical suggestions for doing this will be discussed in due course.

The types and quantity of such errors that emerge in student interlanguages will depend, clearly, on the nature of the differences between NL and SL surface and conceptual systems. Consider the following erroneous sentences that were committed by students of Italian at the University of Toronto in one of my classes during the 1991-1992 academic year:

72. *Io aspetto per Maria ogni giorno* (intended meaning: 'I wait for Mary every day').

73. *Ciao professore, ti vedo domani* ('Good-bye professor, I'll see you tomorrow').

74. *Io sono molto sensibile quando spendo soldi* (intended meaning: 'I'm very sensible when it comes to spending money').

75. *Il gusto del caffè espresso è più che buono; è delizioso* (intended meaning: 'The taste of espresso coffee is more than good; it is delicious').

76. *Io sono caduta in amore un anno fa* (intended meaning: 'I fell in love a year ago').

Example (72) contains an error caused by a difference in surface structure categories. In English, the verb *to wait* is intransitive and thus takes an indirect object preceded by the preposition *for*. In Italian, on the other hand, *aspettare* is a transitive verb and, therefore, takes a direct object without a preposition. Thus, sentence (72) shows negative transfer at the level of surface structure. Sentence (73) contains, needless to say, a purely communicative error—the use of the informal register of address with a professor. The last three examples contain conceptual errors. The students who uttered (74) and (75) assumed that the meanings of *sensibile* and *delizioso* were isomorphic to English *sensible* and *delicious*—but they are not. Example (76) contains an error in reflexivization. The student assumed that the conceptual metaphor [love is a trap] manifests itself in exactly the same way in the surface structure of Italian—but again it does not. In a comprehensive study investigating conceptual errors, Russo (1997) found these to be the most destructive of communication between learners and native speakers, and the most frequent ones in student interlanguages.

The third task facing SL students is learning how to carry out discourse in a conceptually-appropriate fashion. The pedagogy related to this task will also will be discussed in subsequent chapters.

Suffice it to say here that it entails imparting knowledge of how to interconnect meanings in signifying order terms. Consider, for instance, the following sentences:

77. She has fallen from grace within her place of work.
78. That man is a Don Juan.
79. You've got too many fires going; take it a little easier.

To derive meaning from sentence (77), the Biblical narrative relating to the Garden of Eden must be known (at least unconsciously). To understand what is intended in (78) the Don Juan legend must be known. And to extract a meaning from (79) knowledge (at least in part) of a specific proverb must be known. In discourse, such signifieds are constantly interconnected in the delivery of meaning. The learning task in this case can be characterized as a *navigational* one, since the student must learn how to navigate through the network of interconnected meanings that constitute a signifying order.

Comprehensive network analyses and reflexivization training are the central features of the semiotic approach to SLT that has been discussed so far. It is the ability to navigate through the overarching circuitry of all kinds networks, choosing appropriate denotative, connotative, or metaphorical circuits according to communicative need, and integrating them cohesively into appropriate self-fashioned circuitry to match the need, that constitutes conceptual fluency in the SL. The purpose of the next three chapters is to discuss those circuits.

Chapter III
Denotative concepts

3. Introductory remarks

As discussed in the previous chapter, denotative concepts exist in network domains that are forged by the process of *association-by-sense*. Denotation is essentially "dictionary meaning". It is the operative mode in establishing basic concepts in a culture and in carrying out common routine communicative interactions that require formulaic speech (such as greeting, expressing appreciation, etc.). However, statistical studies of discourse reveal consistently that it is a relatively negligible mode for the delivery of most messages intended to have an effect on interlocutors (e.g. Pollio, Barlow, Fine, and Pollio 1977; Ortony 1979; Kövecses 1986, 1988, 1990; Lakoff and Turner 1989).

Denotative networks show a higher degree of compactness than do connotative and metaphorical networks—i.e. the circuits within them show a compact configuration; connotative and metaphorical conceptual networks, on the other hand, show a more diffuse connectivity created by a greater degree of interlinkage with other network domains (grafting). Consider the word *green*—a word that encodes a stretch of hue on the spectrum that has a wavelength of approximately 490 to 570 nanometers. Etymologically, it was probably motivated by observing the hue in *grass* and most *plant leaves*. A denotative analysis of this concept will thus show that it is connected in a compact fashion to only a limited number of key nodes and their offshoot circuits within the *color* network domain. It is connected, of course, with the superordinate node of *color* itself, and is thus part of a circuit that includes, *red, blue, green, yellow,* etc. It is also connected to a *shade* node that generates a circuit which includes such nodes as *light* and *dark*.

As a focal node within the *color* network domain, its denotative structure can be shown as follows:

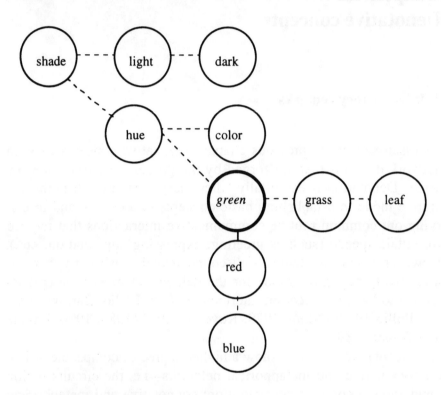

Figure 18. A denotative network for *green*

The semiotic story of *green* is, of course, not complete until the many connotative and metaphorical concepts it entails are interconnected with its meaning. These are found commonly in such expressions as the following:

80. She's *green* with envy.
81. The grass is always *greener* on the other side.
82. He's at the *green* age of eighteen.

This part of the story will be discussed in the next two chapters. Suffice it to say here that adding these nodes to the network above involves considerable inter-network connectivity: The association of *green* with *envy* (80) and *hope* (81) results from a linkage of *color* and *feeling* network domains; the meaning that derives from associating *green* with *youth* (82) results from a linkage of *color* and *age* domains:

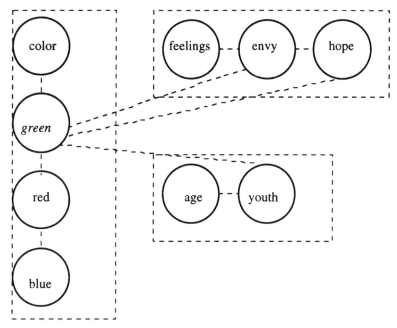

Figure 19. Connotative extensions of *green* through network grafting

3.1 Denotation

Denotation serves, above all else, the function of encoding sense impressions by association: e.g. the color *blue* stands for a visual property observed in the sky and the sea; *green* for a visual property observed in *grass* and *leaves*; and so on. Once a denotative concept enters the language, it then becomes organized associatively, greatly determining a person's perception of specific kinds of referents.

As an example, recall Langacker's notion of noun *boundedness* (chapter 2, §2.2.2). The referents that some nouns encode, Langacker proposed, are characterized by having, or not having, a boundary. A count noun refers to something that either has a boundary or encircles a bounded region; a mass noun refers to something that does not have boundaries nor encircles bounded regions. Thus, for instance, the count noun *book* in English refers to an object that encircles a *bounded* region, whereas the mass noun *salt* refers to something that does not. The grammatical consequences of this conceptual dichotomy include: (1) the fact that *book* can be pluralized (*books*), *salt* cannot (in its denotative sense); (2) the fact that *book* can be preceded by an indefinite article (*a book*), *salt* cannot; (3) the fact that *salt* can be preceded by *a bit of* (*a bit of salt*); *book* cannot; and so on.

Now, the user of such words will perceive certain referents in specific ways. However, such encoding is not universal. Comparing Italian and English nouns in terms of the *boundedness* feature reveals that, occasionally, the two languages encode the same referents in dissimilar ways. And this, in turn, becomes a source for conceptual errors, as can be detected in the following sentences produced by Italian-speaking students at the University of Perugia where I was a visiting professor during the 1998 academic year:

83. *I have many *informations* to tell.
84. *I do not like *grape*; I prefer bananas.

Sentence (83) shows an error in pluralization that is traceable to the fact that *informazione* ('information') in Italian is encoded denotatively as referring to something *bounded*. For this reason, it has a plural form in Italian. The corresponding English form *information* does not because it encodes an *unbounded* referent. Sentence (84) shows the opposite type of error. The referent encoded by the Italian word *uva* ('grapes') is perceived as *unbounded*. For this reason it cannot be pluralized in its surface form, whereas the corresponding English word *grape* can, because it is perceived as encoding a *bounded* referent.

As the above examples show, surface differences between languages are caused by differences in conceptualization. As further proof of this general observation, consider the following two Italian sentences:

85. *Sapevo che arrivava ieri* ('I knew he was arriving yesterday').
86. *Ho saputo che è arrivato ieri* ('I found out he arrived yesterday').

Comparing these sentences with their English counterparts shows the following contrast. Italian encodes 'knowing' with one signifier, *sapere*, reflexivizing the difference between 'knowing' and 'knowing for sure' as a tense dichotomy—i.e. the former is rendered by the imperfect form of the verb (*sapevo*) and the latter by the present perfect form (*ho saputo*). English, on the other hand, has encoded the two referents with separate words, thus assigning a separate conceptual status to each one. This difference is the source of conceptual errors such as the following ones committed by two of the Perugia students:

    87. *I *have known* that she called yesterday.
    88. *I *was knowing* that they were studying.

As such conceptual errors show, differences in denotation do not constitute simple differences in form; rather, they entail differences in conceptualization that show up in anomalous surface structures. Clearly, describing and documenting the relevant differences in the domain of denotation will constitute an important task of applied semiotics.

3.1.1 Encoding denotative concepts

Encoding denotative concepts entails knowing how to use the surface codes (grammar and vocabulary) for this purpose. This implies two general abilities—the ability to recognize and produce SL signifiers at a purely physical level and the ability to apply them to reflect conceptual properties. This is equivalent to the ability of the musician to distinguish among the different tones of a scale, or to the ability of the painter to distinguish among lines, shapes, textures, colors, etc., in view of their uses in their respective art forms.

    Consider the iconic deployment of a language's phonemic system to model certain kinds of referents. In English the sounds made by a snake, for example, are encoded (in part) by signifiers composed with the cluster /sl/—e.g. *slides, slips by*, etc. In Italian, on the other hand, the palatal phoneme /š/ is used for the same descriptive purpose—e.g. *strusciare, strisciare*, etc. Minimal differences of this type abound between languages. Here are a few examples of inbuilt iconicity in English and Italian words:

Table 1.   Phonemic iconicity in English and Italian

English	Italian
to neigh	*nitrire*
to bark	*abbaiare*
to meow	*miagolare*
to chirp	*cinquettare*
to moo	*muggire*

Prosody also constitutes a source for encoding denotative concepts. While in English tonal distinction is not critical in conceptualization, it is, for instance, in North Mandarin Chinese in which numerous concepts are distinguished by differences in the rise and fall of tone. The single syllable /ma/, for example, can have various meanings according to whether the tone is level (—), rising (↑), dipping (↕) or falling (↓):

89. /ma —/   'mother'
90. /ma ↑/   'hemp'
91. /ma ↕/   'horse'
92. /ma ↓/   'scold'

In English, tone is used for a different reason – to signal differences in discourse function. Statements, for instance, end with a falling intonation pattern; whereas some types of questions – e.g. those that can be answered with a *yes* or a *no* – end with a rising intonation pattern:

93. Do you speak English? (↑)
94. Do you know Ms. Jones? (↑)

Depending on language, it is obvious that SL students face the task of learning how new and unfamiliar surface codes and subcodes represent conceptual structures differentially. In the area of morphology, this entails recognizing the parts of a word that encode specific kinds of meanings. A word is known more technically as a *minimal free form*. But not all words are free forms. For instance, *unthinkable* is decomposable into smaller units that also have meaning: (1) the basic free form, *think*, which has a lexical meaning; (2) the negative prefix *un-* which has a recurring functional meaning ('opposite of'), and (3) the suffix *-able* which also has a functional meaning ('the act or process of being something').

The task faced by the SL learner consists in recognizing how to segment words in conceptually appropriate ways Take, for instance, the following forms found in Swahili, a northern Bantu (African) language:

95.	*nitasoma*	'I will read'
96.	*nilisoma*	'I read (past)'
97.	*utasoma*	'you will read'
98.	*ulisoma*	'you read (past)'

By comparing these forms systematically, it is possible to establish the following morphemic facts. Since /-soma/ occurs in all four, it can be deduced to be a lexical morpheme that has a meaning corresponding to English 'read'. Comparing the first two forms, (95) and (96), against the last two, (97) and (98), it can be seen that the morpheme /ni-/ corresponds to the English pronoun 'I' and /u-/ to the pronoun 'you'. Comparing the first and second forms in tandem with the third and fourth, it can be deduced that /-ta-/ is a future tense grammatical morpheme and /-li-/ a past tense grammatical morpheme. This contrastive glossing technique is reflective of what students typically do as they attempt to figure out the meanings of new input

The encoding of denotative meaning entails classification. As a concrete example, consider the Italian words below:

99. *padre* ('father'), *madre* ('mother'), *figlio* ('son'), *figlia* ('daughter')

100. *bue* ('ox'), *mucca* ('cow'), *vitello* ('male calf'), *vitella* (female calf, heifer')

101.   *cane* ('male dog'), *cagna* ('female dog'), *cagnolino*
('male puppy'), *cagnolina* ('female puppy')

If these are compared to words such as *pane* ('bread'), *latte* ('milk'), *spada* ('sword'), *auto* ('car'), etc. it can easily be seen that they all share the property of *animacy*. Hence, this feature would appear to be a basic one in establishing their denotative meaning. Now, comparing the items in (99) with those in (100) and (101) it is easy to see that they are kept distinct by the feature *human*; and comparing (100) and (101) reveals that a further distinction has been encoded – namely, *bovine* vs. *canine*. These are, in effect, conceptual nodes within separate denotative networks. Finally, what keeps the words in the three networks distinct are the features *adult, youth, male*, and *female*. The associative structure implicit in the concepts encoded in (99) can be shown as follows:

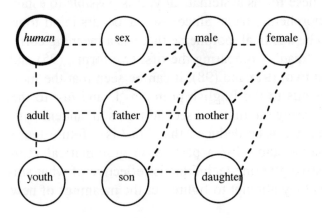

Figure 20. Part of the network domain for *human*

The respective network domains for *bovine* and *canine* will show the exact same type of configuration. Note that categories such as *animate*, *human*, *bovine*, and *canine* are superordinate concepts; while the words *padre, madre, figlio, figlia*, etc. are basic level concepts.

The following chart shows which distinctive features are possessed by each word in its conceptual make-up:

Table 2.   Distinctive-feature analysis of various words

	animate	human	bovine	canine	adult	male	female
padre	+	+	+	+	+	+	-
madre	+	+	-	-	+	-	+
figlio	+	+	-	-	-	+	-
figlia	+	+	-	-	-	-	+
bue	+	-	+	-	+	+	-
mucca	+	-	+	-	+	-	+
vitello	+	-	+	-	-	+	-
vitella	+	-	+	-	-	-	+
cane	+	-	-	+	+	+	-
cagna	+	-	-	+	+	-	+
cagnolino	+	-	-	+	-	+	-
cagnolina	+	-	-	+	-	-	+

Although this is a useful way of establishing the denotative meaning of lexical items, it can lead to problems. The opposition above between *vitella* and *cagna* can be given as either *bovine* vs. *canine* or as *canine* vs. *bovine*. There really is no way to establish which one is, psychologically, the actual trigger in the opposition. Moreover, when certain words are defined in terms of such features, it becomes obvious that to keep them distinct one will need quite a vast array of them. The whole exercise would thus become artificial and convoluted. Such problems are avoided by the use of network diagrams that show how the concepts are associated to each other within and across domains.

3.1.2 Reflexivizing denotative concepts

Reflexivization involves knowledge of how grammar and vocabulary convert associative conceptual structure into linear surface structure. Consider, for example, the relation between an active and passive sentence such as *Alex ate the apple* vs. *The apple was eaten by Alex*.

Conceptually, the two sentences encode a different perspective of the action of *eating*. In the active sentence, the subject (*Alex*), which is the first form in the sentence, encodes an image of the referent (*Alex*) as being in the *foreground* with respect to the *apple*, which is visualized mentally as being in the *background*. This is due to the presence of a *view* node in the conceptual structure of transitive verbs—in the above sentence the action (*eating*) is viewable as an activity in which the subject is its "perpetrator" or "executor" and, thus, as being in the *foreground*:

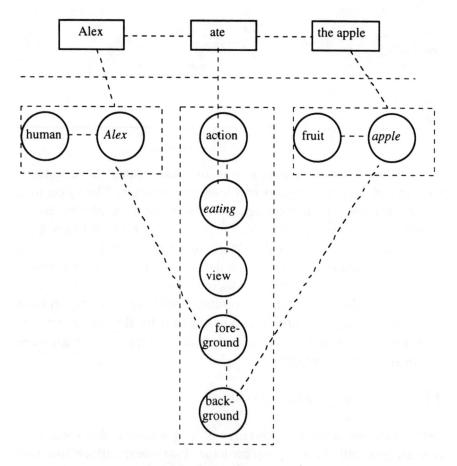

Figure 21. Reflexivizing an active sentence

A change in conceptual structure changes the order of the words in the surface structure. The passive sentence brings the object to the *foreground*, relegating the subject to the *background*. The action of eating is now viewable as an activity in which the object is its "receiver". The different morphemic reflexivization of the verb also encodes the new conceptual view from which to examine the action:

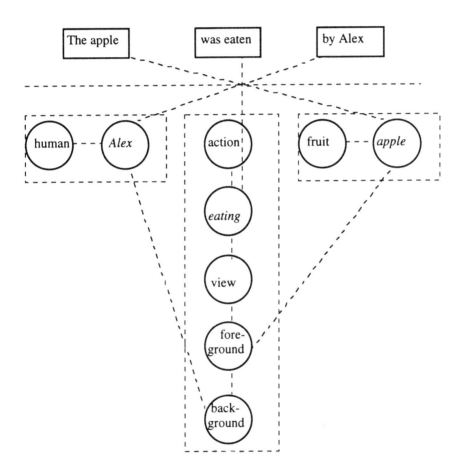

Figure 22. Reflexivizing a passive sentence

Sometimes, surface forms in isolation (i.e. without a context) produce ambiguity, because they reflexivize different conceptual structures in certain ways. As we saw in chapter 1 (§1.4.1), a sentence such as *The pig is ready to eat* can have various meanings, depending on the social context in which it is uttered. Now, consider the following two sentences:

    102. Easy does it all the time.
    103. The chair is over there.

Example (102) can be interpreted as a variant to *It is always best to take it easy*; but if one is told that *Easy* is a person, then it takes on a different meaning. Similarly (103) has two meanings depending on the concept that *chair* encodes—a 'seat' or a 'person'. Such contextual information is, clearly, critical in determining the meaning of sentences. The conceptual structure of (102) would show *easy* either as a node in a circuit generated by a superordinate *behavior* node; or as a node in a circuit generated by a superordinate node *name*; the conceptual structure of (103) would show *chair* either as a node in a circuit generated by a superordinate *seat* node; or as a node in a circuit generated by a superordinate *human* node.

One common source of ambiguity is *homonymy*. Homonyms are words or phrases with the same pronunciation and/or spelling, but with different meanings. If the homonymy is purely phonetic then the items are known as *homophones* (e.g. *aunt* vs. *ant* and *bore* vs. *boar*). If the homonymy is orthographic, then the words are known as *homographs* (*play* as in *Shakespeare's play* vs. *play* as in *He likes to play*). It is not the case that all homographs are homophones: e.g. the form *learned* has two pronunciations in *He learned to play the violin* vs. *He is a learned man*.

Surface forms that encode the same concept are known as *synonyms*—e.g. *near-close, far-distant*, etc. However, there virtually never is a case of *pure synonymy*. Take, for instance, *near* and *close*. Ignoring nuances of meaning for the sake of argument, in the following sentences, the two are interpretable as virtually synonymous:

    104. My house is *near* the mall.
    105. My house is *close* to the mall.

However, when the referents that follow them in sentences are marked as *animate* then synonymy is not always a possibility. Sentences (106) and (107) below show that the two do not completely overlap in range of application and are thus not pure synonyms.

106. Mary and I have been *close* for years (= connotative meaning).
107. *Mary and I have been *near* for years (= connotative meaning).
108. I want to get *near* to Mary, but she won't let me (= denotative meaning).
109. I want to get *close* to Mary, but she won't let me (= denotative meaning).

The substitution of *near* in (107) for *close* (106) is anomalous because of it has not been grafted onto the *animate* network domain through connotative extension. The counterpart of synonymy is *antonymy*. Antonyms are words that are felt to be opposite in meaning—*night*-day, *sad-happy, hot-cold, good-bad*, etc. But antonymy, like synonymy, depends on underlying conceptual features. Consider the use of *far* as an antonym for *near* and *close*:

110. My house is *far* from the mall
111. Mary and I have been *far apart* for years.
112. I want to get *far away* from Mary, but she won't let me.

In (110) the substitution of *far* produces no surface structure adjustment. However, both its use in (111) and (112) entails the use of additional lexical material—i.e. *apart* and *away*.

Substitution can occur across sentences in surface structure assemblages. The function of such substitution is to maintain the smooth flow of discourse. Consider, for instance, the following two accounts, which tell the same story in different ways:

113. Mary went to the store yesterday. Mary met a friend at the store. Mary and the friend greeted each other. Mary hadn't seen her friend in a long time.

114. Mary went to the store yesterday. She met a friend
      at the store. They greeted each other. Mary hadn't
      seen her in a long time.

The first one sounds stilted and odd, even though by itself, each
sentence in it is well-formed. The second version reads more like ordinary conversation because in English, as in other languages, repetition is discouraged in normal discourse. For this reason, the surface
code makes available several devices that allow for the same information to be reflexivized without the repetition.

Devices that refer back to some word or syntactic category are
called *anaphoric*. In (114) above, *she* refers back to *Mary*, *they* to
Mary and the friend, and *her* to *her friend*. The opposite of an anaphoric device is a *cataphoric* one. This is a word or particle used in
anticipation of some other word. For example, in the sentence *Even if
he denies it, I swear that Mark did it*, the pronoun *he* refers ahead to
Mark. Subject and object pronouns, locative particles, demonstra-
tives, adverbs, for instance, often function as anaphoric and cataphoric particles in conversations and narrative texts.

3.2 Denotative discourse

The aim of the communicative methodologists was to move away
from *langue* as the focus of instruction to *parole*, claiming that, like
an organism, language is a highly adaptive and context-sensitive in-
strument that is shaped by forces that are largely external to it. The
rules of grammar, they emphasized, are highly susceptible to the
subtle influences that the discourse situation in which they are used
has on them. The internal structures of language are pliable entities
that are responsive to social situations. *Langue* and *parole* are really
two sides of the same coin, rather than separate dimensions (Spolsky
1998).

This basic idea is, of course, a valid one semiotically, since discourse involves *text-construction*—a process that involves converting
conceptual structures into surface syntax for the purpose of carrying
out pragmatic functions (saying hello, wishing someone well, etc.),

solving problems of communication, and utilizing the register or level of formality that is appropriate to a given situation. The aim of applied semiotics is not to describe the latter aspects of discourse. These have been studied extensively. Its aim, rather, is to describe how discourse reflects conceptual structure.

Parenthetically, it might be mentioned that among the various theoretical models put forward over the years to describe the psychology of discourse, the one by the Moscow-born linguist and semiotician who carried out most of his work in the United States, Roman Jakobson (1960), is perhaps the most insightful one and is therefore worth summarizing here. Jakobson posited six "constituents" that characterize all speech acts:

- an *addresser* who initiates a communication;

- an *addressee* who is the intended receiver of the message;

- a *message* that the addresser and the addressee recognize must refer to something other than itself;

- a *context* that permits the addressee to recognize that a message is referring to something other than itself: e.g. if someone were crying out *Help*, lying motionless on the ground, then one would easily understand that the message is referring to a plea for assistance;

- a mode of *contact* by which a message is delivered (the physical channel) and the primary social and psychological connections that are established between the addresser and addressee;

- a *code* providing the signs and structural patterns for constructing and deciphering messages;

Jakobson then pointed out that each of these constituents deter-
mines a different communicative function:

- *emotive*, which acknowledges that a primary function
  of discourse is to allow an addresser to convey emotions, attitudes, social status, etc. in the message;

- *conative*, which acknowledges that another main
  function of discourse is to produce an effect—
  physical, psychological, social, etc.—on an addressee;

- *referential*, which acknowledges that another function
  of discourse is to convey information (*Main Street is
  two blocks away*);

- *poetic*, which acknowledges that an additional function of discourse is to deliver meanings effectively
  through rhyme, rhythm, etc. (*Roses are red, violets
  are blue, something tells me that you like me too*);

- *phatic*, which acknowledges that yet another function
  of discourse is to establish social contact (*Hi, how's it
  going?*);

- *metalingual*, which acknowledges that one more
  function of discourse is to refer to the code used (*The
  word noun is a noun*).

Communication between two people is not a simple transfer of
information, as Jakobson argued. Above all else, most of human discourse is laden with connotative and metaphorical meanings, and
thus highly *poetic* in function, as we shall discuss in the next two
chapters.

3.2.1 Discourse structure

Consider the following common scenarios in which a 17-year-old male high school student says good-bye (circa 1998), first to his English teacher, second to his mother, and third to a peer:

115. *To his English teacher*:
     Good-bye, sir!

116. *To his mother*:
     See ya' later, ma!

117. *To a peer*:
     I gotta' split, man!

Clearly, these are not interchangeable utterances—i.e. the adolescent would not say *I gotta' split, man!* to a teacher, and vice versa, he would not say, *Good-bye, sir!* to a peer. This simple, yet instructive example, shows that the choice of language forms and the types of structural patterns that are utilized in specific situations will vary predictably. This kind of practical knowledge is clearly different from the knowledge of structural relations in themselves. It involves knowing *who* says *what* to *whom* in specific situations.

The objective of communicative syllabi was to emphasize speech situations, identifying which target surface forms would be used in them, so that students could carry out such emotive, conative, referential, and phatic functions as initiating and ending contact, thanking, congratulating, showing satisfaction, approving, disapproving, showing surprise, offering to do something, renouncing, suggesting, warning, begging, exchanging facts, reporting, comparing, asking for opinions, keeping track of time, expressing spatial relations, self portrayal, explicating family relations, getting angry, arguing, reacting to statements, ordering, and demanding. Although much leeway was given in communicative syllabi in the linguistic choices that could be made to match a function, rarely did such syllabi show a relation between surface and conceptual structure in discourse.

The critical aspect for applied semiotics is that the words that constitute speech choices are reflexes conceptual circuitry that has been constructed from the resources of the signifying order in order to successfully carry out a speech act. The above three ways of saying good-bye show the following underlying circuitry:

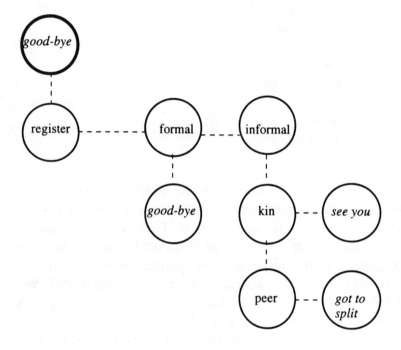

Figure 23. Conceptual structure of *good-bye*

Although the origin of *got to split* is metaphorical, it is included here to round out the description. Needless to say, the above diagram shows only a fragment of the entire network for *leave-taking*. The thing to note is that the ability to choose the appropriate node in an appropriate social manner entails knowing how to *navigate* (chapter 2, §2.3.) through the many interconnected networks that are made available by the signifying order.

As another example, consider the verbal strategy known as a *gambit*. A gambit is a word or phrase used to open a conversation, to keep it going, to make it flow smoothly, etc. In English, for example, the following are gambits with three different functions:

118. Uh huh...ya...hmm...aha...
119. You agree with me, don't you?
120. May I ask you a question?

The grunt-like expression uttered in (118) constitutes a gambit for acknowledging that one is listening to an interlocutor, especially on the phone. Total silence is not an appropriate gambit in English conversation, although it is in other languages. In Italian a different gambit is deployed for this function, namely a series of words such as, *sì...capisco...eh già...vero...* The gambit in (119) is known as a tag question (literally a question tagged on at the end of a sentence). It is designed in (119) as an agreement-seeking strategy. The gambit in (120) is a conversation opener. The network from which these gambits are taken would contain these nodes:

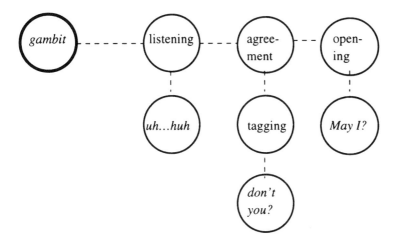

Figure 24. Conceptual structure of different gambits

In a more detailed network analysis the various secondary and tertiary circuits generated by the above nodes would also be shown.

Thus, for instance, the *tagging* node would be shown to generate a circuit containing such forms as *OK?, Right?, You agree?*, etc. These are found commonly reflexivized at the end of sentences:

121. Excuse me, I'm in the right place, *aren't I?*
122. You agree, *don't you?*
123. You like it too, *right?*

Networks also exist for the purpose of repairing conversation breakdowns. Phrases such as *Excuse me* or *Sorry,* for example, are part of such networks. Also part of discourse structure are the gestures that accompany conversation, as we shall see in chapter 5. These may seem to be disconnected to the language used, but a closer analysis reveals that they are highly interconnected with it. Although there are cross-cultural similarities in gesture, substantial differences also exist both in the extent to which it is used and in the interpretations given to its particular forms. For example, the head gestures for *yes* and *no* used in the Balkans seem inverted to other Europeans. In 1979, the anthropologist Desmond Morris, together with several of his associates at Oxford University, examined 20 gestures in 40 different areas of Europe—publishing the results in a widely-quoted book titled *Gestures: Their Origins and Distributions.* The research team found some rather fascinating things. For instance, they discovered that many of the gestures had several meanings, depending on culture: e.g. a tap on the side of the head can indicate completely opposite things—'stupidity' or 'intelligence'—according to cultural context. They also found that most of the gestural signifiers were used in many countries.

As a final example of how discourse network structure influences surface form, consider variation in language. In northern Italy, for instance, there is a tendency to use the present perfect to describe virtually all past actions—e.g. *Sono andato al cinema la settimana scorsa* 'I went to the movies last week'. In many parts of southern Italy, especially in Sicily, the tendency is, instead, to use the past absolute—*Andai al cinema la settimana scorsa.* Referring to a watermelon as *cocomero, anguria,* or *melone* also falls along dialectal lines: *cocomero* is used primarily in central and south-central parts of Italy, *anguria* in northern Italy, and *melone* in many parts of southern

Italy. Such variation is an intrinsic part of Italian discourse structure. Such subtle differences can be found in networks that are interconnected in various overlapping and crisscrossing ways The *watermelon* network can be represented (in highly simplified form) as follows:

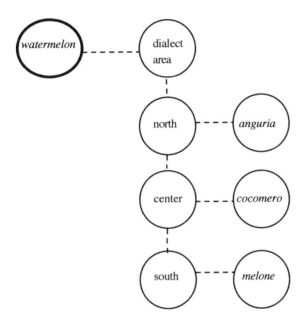

Figure 25. A dialect network for *watermelon* in Italian

Some variation networks develop due to the class and group divisions within a society. For example, in England, members of certain social groups often adopt a particular pronunciation of /h/ as a way of distinguishing themselves from other social groups. Similarly, the inhabitants of Martha's Vineyard, in Massachusetts, have adopted particular vowel pronunciations to distinguish themselves from people vacationing on the island.

3.2.3 Navigation

One of the main tasks facing SLA learners is, clearly, learning how to *navigate* (chapter 2, §2.3) through discourse networks in order to forge the appropriate conceptual structure of the text required to deliver a specific speech function. Obviously, knowledge of the entire web of interconnecting networks in discourse is something that no one knows. But the crucial point is that *they can be learned* as required. Many networks are formed as a result of specialized needs—e.g. networks pertaining to medical discourse, sports discourse, etc. It is obvious that the greater the knowledge of network circuitry, the greater the ability to negotiate meaning and, in many cases, to control the flow of discourse. Great orators are persuasive speakers because they are expert navigators of discourse networks and great makers of effective textual circuitry. Listening to them is equivalent to taking an exciting journey through the many domains of meaning that a signifying order makes available—no matter how hypocritical or opportunistic the purpose of the journey.

Learners typically construct SL discourse texts on the basis of NL networks and circuits. This is why their discourse flow is often anomalous—it is guided by NL circuitry. Needless to say, areas of network isomorphism produce discourse texts that are indistinguishable from native-speaker ones; areas of overlap and differentiation, on the other hand, lead to the creation of texts that are constructed with the surface structure forms of the SL, but the discourse structure of the NL.

A pedagogically-useful distinction in the domain of discourse analysis is the one between *discourse network* and a *discourse path*. A network is a system of nodes and circuits that are available for constructing a type of text or part of a text. Thus, a network of gambits would contain all the nodes and circuits that allow native speakers to utilize them in discourse to fit a situation. Any specific navigation through this network is the *path* chosen for some specific purpose. Drawing paths allows one to see how networks have been utilized. Consider, for instance, the following stretch of discourse:

> You believe me, don't you? I tell ya' that she is a really
> horrible person. Because of her, the others have been able
> to do as they please. I can't believe it!

The path diagram of this text will show the following configuration:

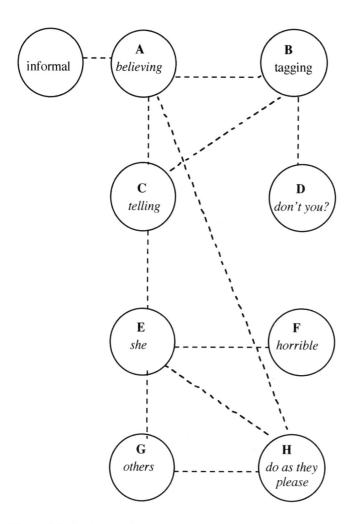

Figure 26. Path analysis of a discourse text

There are several things to note about this path diagram:

- Node **A** leads in two directions: (1) to **B,** which is a tagging strategy, which in turn has its own circuit **A-B**, and (2) to **C.**

- **E** is connected to four circuits: **E-C**, **E-F**, **E-G**, and **E-B**, because the topic of the text—*she*—is connected to the *others*, who *do as they please*, because of *her*, and this is what is *horrible*.

- Node **C** is connected as well to the tagging strategy, as is obvious in the discourse text.

- Finally, nodes **A** and **B** form a circuit, since it must be *believed* that the *others do as they please*.

Path analysis provides a glimpse, so to speak, into the meandering, twisting, yet cohesive structure of discourse events. It thus aims to show how we extract *sense* from strings of words, not as a "sum of their meanings", but as related to each other in associative ways. A path diagram is not a replica of "what happens in the mind", of course; it is simply a graphic sketch designed to show the conceptual structure of a discourse event. The reflexivization of such circuitry often functions as an "editing system", so to speak, filtering out repetitions through anaphora, cataphora, conjunction, etc., and thus "putting the finishing touches" to the physical form of discourse.

Reflexivization also allows a speaker to encode feelings, emphases, or point of view in specific ways. Recall from chapter 2 (§2.2.2) that adjectives in Italian can, sometimes, be put before nouns rather than after. In many cases this creates a different conceptual emphasis in discourse:

124. *Lui è un nuovo amico* ('He is a new friend' *with emphasis*).
125. *Lui è un amico nuovo* ('He's a new friend' *without emphasis*).

Sentence (124) emphasizes the *newness* concept more than the *friendship* one. In terms of the underlying circuitry of discourse, (126) would show a circuit in which *nuovo* is a generating node and *amico* one of the offshoot nodes in the circuit; (125) would show a reverse structure.

3.3 Pedagogical considerations

The traditional SLT approaches have produced some rather effective techniques for imparting denotative modes of conceptualization and discourse. In an applied semiotic framework, however, the focus would be put on differences in conceptual circuitry and on the re-flexivization processes that encode them. In this framework, how-ever, the notion of syllabus can be seen to have no foreseeable use. This notion was a consequence of the widely-held twentieth century view in psychology that language is learned according to an "internal clock", so to speak, present in all learners. But, whether or not this is true, its incorporation into SLT has, as we saw in chapter 1, rarely produced truly effective outcomes. This does not mean that the kinds of information that both the structural and communicative syllabi contained are no longer pedagogically useful. On the contrary, they contain many practical insights into how conceptual reorganization and navigation can be nurtured and facilitated in many areas of SLA. But the *sequence* of learning cannot be predicted because, as argued in this book, conceptual structure is associative in nature, not linear. The emergence of higher degrees of conceptual fluency will thus de-pend on how much opportunities the student has had to forge rele-vant conceptual associations.

Extremely useful are the many suggestions for carrying out sur-face-structure practice in the classroom that the methods employed:

- *Mechanical exercises*. These provide an opportunity for the students to control the features of surface structure separately from the conceptual system: e.g. putting nouns into the plural, inserting the correct form of the article in form of a noun, making adjec-tives agree with nouns, conjugating verbs, multiple-choice exercises, substitution exercises, etc.

- *Meaningful exercises.* These provide an opportunity for the students to link surface structure with conceptual structure: e.g. translation exercises, filling-in blanks with appropriate words, cloze techniques, reading SL texts, etc.

- *Applicational exercises.* These provide both the structure and communicative contexts in which texts can be constructed or modified: e.g. paraphrasing or modifying texts in certain specific ways.

From the communicative syllabus the following techniques can also be seen to be effective for imparting denotative competence. In all instances, the teacher would have to make sure that conceptual fluency is the focus of the task (through intervention, illustration, explanation, etc.):

- *Closed communication tasks.* These involve getting students to perform certain functions: e.g. Order the following beverages (coffee, tea, etc.); Make a deposit at a bank of $500 dollars; etc.

- *Open communication tasks.* These are more open-ended, allowing students freer usage of the SL: e.g. Ask the person next to you what her favorite music is and why.

- *Identification tasks.* These require students to identify specific facts of SL input. e.g. What is the name of the person ordering coffee in the dialogue? Where does he come from? etc.

- *Function-related tasks.* These involve getting students to relate surface form to discourse networks:: e.g.

Form questions asking the following things—where Mary is, what Armando is doing tonight, etc.

- *Personalized tasks*. These involve getting the learners to express personal points of view in a controlled manner: e.g. Say whether you do or do not like the current President of the United States and why.

- *Information-giving tasks*. These involve getting students to use the SL to convey information: e.g. Say what kind of dwelling you live in; Give your address; etc.

- *Information-getting tasks*. These involve getting students to use the SL to get information: e.g. Ask a partner what radio or TV program he/she likes best and why.

- *Cultural identification tasks*. These require students to recognize certain facts about the SL culture: e.g. Give the Italian for each of the following—five well-known movie directors, five great artists, etc.

- *Cloze tasks*. These require students to supply words that were systematically deleted from a text.

- *Description tasks*. These require students to describe certain things or people: Describe what your mother is likely to wear to work.

- *Class discussion tasks*. These involve getting students to interact through discussion or debate: e.g. How much time do you spend watching TV each day? Why?

- *Open-ended completion tasks*. These require students to finish certain statements logically: e.g. The dollar is diminishing because...

- *Problem-solving tasks*. These require students to solve problems of communication: e.g. What is wrong with the statement *Ciao professore*?

The emphasis in a semiotic classroom would, of course, be on network and path analyses. These can be used to teach or explain new material directly. I have used such analyses to impart writing fluency to SL students. The method I have used consists of the following components:

- Students are asked to write down their ideas in their NL in any fashion they desire: i.e. they are asked to indicate *what* they want to say in the composition.

- They are then asked to connect the ideas among themselves by drawing a path diagram.

- Through contrastive analysis, these diagrams are then revised to portray nodes and circuits that are consistent with SL discourse structure. This component requires analysis of similar texts composed by native speakers, the use of reference materials (dictionaries, thesauruses, etc.), and intervention by the teacher with direct coaching.

- After a path analysis has been completed, then the students are required to list the grammatical and lexical resources available to them for reflexivizing the path. This component also requires the use of reference materials and intervention by the teacher.

- The students then write the composition and asked to edit it appropriately after commentary by the teacher.

- Finally, the students are required to write the final version of the composition.

The above method of instruction was used with two experimental classes during the 1997 and 1998 academic years. One class was at the University of Lugano and consisted of Italian-speaking students studying English as a second language; the other was at the University of Toronto and consisted of English-speaking students studying Italian as a second language. Altogether, 123 compositions were written by these students. I then gave these to native-speaking colleagues to assess them for their conceptual appropriateness: i.e. I gave the English compositions to professional colleagues whose native language was English and the Italian ones to colleagues whose native language was Italian. Except for a few cases, the colleagues generally found them to be superior to the usual compositions that foreign-language students write. Although this in no way constitutes a controlled experiment, it nevertheless provided some indication that conceptual fluency could be imparted in a classroom situation.

The discussion in this and the pervious chapter also makes it obvious that an expanded use of contrastive analysis (CA) will be necessary. CA was developed by audiolingual methodologists in order to determine what target and native language structures were similar and different in order to organize the teaching syllabus according to a simple learning principle—areas of similarity require less instructional emphasis and can be assumed to be acquired spontaneously, while areas showing differences require attention proportional to the degree of difference.

In its original form, therefore, CA came to be accepted both as a theory of SLA and as an organizing principle around which to plan for language teaching. As Stern (1983: 46) aptly put it: "Contrastive

Analysis was not intended to offer a new method of teaching; but it was a form of language description which was particularly applicable to curriculum development, the preparation and evaluation of teaching materials, to the diagnosis of learning problems, and to testing". CA methodologists viewed the NL as a "filter" that was used by the learner for deciphering target language input.

It was the structural linguist Charles Fries (1927, 1945) who developed CA during the 1940s, claiming that the unconscious transfer of NL grammatical and lexical patterns to the learning of the SL produces characteristic errors in those areas where such patterns are divergent or nonexistent. In so doing, Fries founded applied linguistics as an autonomous branch of general linguistics. After Fries' (1945) and, a little later, Lado's (1957) establishment of the basic principles of CA a widely-acclaimed book series edited by Charles A. Ferguson was published by the University of Chicago Press (Kufner 1962; Stockwell and Bowen 1965a, 1965b; Agard and Di Pietro 1965a, 1965b), which demonstrated that CA was flexible enough to reflect changing views of language design.

In the 1960s and 1970s, transfer theory was abruptly abandoned. In part, this was caused by the association of CA with linguistic structuralism and psychological behaviorism, which became a stigmatic one during those two decades. In larger part, it was caused by the all-encompassing nature of the theory itself. By simply providing a taxonomy of linguistic contrasts, CA was thought to be capable of predicting the corresponding taxonomy of difficulties a learner would encounter on account of NL interference.

The unworkability of this general model of SLA is now a well-documented fact. As Wardhaugh (1970) pointed out over two decades ago, in its original, or *strong*, version CA was unrealistic because it claimed to be an *a priori* predictive theory of learning difficulties. He suggested, however, that a more acceptable, *weaker* version would explain difficulties on an *a posteriori* basis. It was the late Robert J. Di Pietro (1971) who resuscitated interest in the weaker version in the 1970s. By the 1980s, CA was expanded to encompass discourse analysis (e.g. James 1980; Fisiak 1981).

The 1970s and early 1980s also saw the emergence of *error analysis* (chapter 1, §1.1.4). Errors in student interlanguages were explained by error analysts as due to gaps in linguistic and/or communicative competence (e.g. Richards 1971, 1975; Corder 1971; Nemser 1971; Selinker 1972). The regular appearance of such forms as *he goed* and *she comed* in the interlanguages of foreign students of English could not be explained by transfer theory. These were explainable, rather, as resulting from overgeneralization—i.e. from the tendency to apply a rule learned previously to all the items of a linguistic category. Some SLA researchers (e.g. Dulay, Burt, and Krashen 1982) went so far as to claim that all errors, including those thought previously to have been caused by transfer, were the result of over- and undergeneralization. Others saw transfer and generalization as interacting sources of interlanguage errors. As Sridhar (1981: 232) put it: "Interlanguage takes all three systems into account, explicitly incorporating the contrastive analysis of the learner's Interlanguage with both his native and the target language, the difference being that, in interlanguage, the contrastive analysis is an initial filtering device, making way for the testing of hypotheses about the other determinants of the learner's language" (see also Norrish 1983; Robinett and Schachter 1983; Faerch, Haastrup, and Phillipson 1984).

In the past CA and *Error analysis* were used to detect and diagnose structural and communicative errors. But their main value is not in the analysis of surface structure differences. Rather, in my view, the study of conceptual errors is much more valuable since, as Russo (1997) found out, they are the most prevalent ones statistically in interlanguages. The reason for this is the fact that the student's native conceptual system is "the only system in previous experience upon which the learner can draw", as Brown (1987: 177) has so aptly put it.

Chapter IV
Connotative concepts

4. Introductory remarks

The role of connotation in discourse and its interconnectedness to the other networks and circuits of the signifying order has hardly ever been contemplated by the mainstream approaches to SL education. This notwithstanding, a simple examination of discourse texts, *of any kind*, reveals that connotation and metaphor constitute central features in their make-up (Pollio, Barlow, Fine, and Pollio 1977). Connotation is, as discussed previously (chapter 2, §2.1.2), an extensional process, whereby a sign's referent is extended to encompass larger and larger domains of meaning.

Take, a an example, the English word *drop*. The denotative signified of this word is 'falling', as in *He dropped the ball*. Now, this very same signifier can be applied to abstract referents or referential domains that are felt, by extension, to involve imaginary 'falling':

126. There was a considerable *drop* in prices last year.
127. The troops were *dropped* by parachute.
128. I feel like I am going to *drop* dead from exhaustion.
129. I think he has already *dropped* off to sleep.
130. Why don't you let the matter *drop*?
131. Let me *drop* a hint for you.
132. You should *drop* that word from your sentence.
133. She should try not to *drop* behind.

Such common extensional occurrences show that language begets its representational power from the fact that it is largely an extensional modeling system, permitting human beings to encompass increasingly larger and more abstract domains of reference with a finite number of forms. It is this inbuilt feature of language that makes SLA a particularly difficult and complex process. The conceptual reorganization involved in the realm of connotation is highly complicated and time-consuming. Moreover, in the domain of discourse, navigating through connotative circuits in an appropriate manner constitutes developing a knowledge base that encompasses knowledge of the signifying order. The purpose of this chapter will not discuss the main features of connotative conceptualization in a schematic way.

4.1 Connotation

The above example of connotative extensionality can be analyzed more formally in network terms as follows. The concept of 'physical falling', which constitutes a node in the *drop* network allows users of the sign to determine if a specific real or imaginary referent in some other network domain can be connected to it through *association-by inference*. The 'falling' node in English has been connected, for example, to *prices*—example (126) above—because the relative concept created by the association is understandable as a type of 'falling' in numerical terms, i.e. from *higher* values to *lower* ones. This imaginary dropping is, in fact, the conceptual link that undergirds the use of *drop* in all the above examples: e.g. in (127) the position of the airplane is higher than that of the ground, so that troops can be imagined as being *dropped*; in (128) standing is perceivable as referring to a higher position of the body than it is when it is lying down, so that exhaustion can be imagined as a dropping from standing to lying; and so on.

Connotation can be defined, formally, as the extension of a sign's denotative signified to cover new referential domains, if any referent in the new domains is recognizable by association as possessing one or more of the conceptual nodes that define the sign. The application of *drop* in the examples above implies a 'falling' of various kinds by inferential thinking. The connotative structure underlying the use of *drop* in (127), (128), and (129), for example, can be shown as follows:

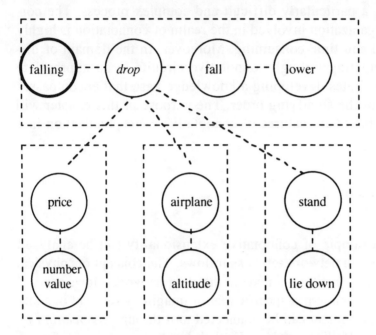

Figure 27. Network analysis of some of the connotations of *drop*

In theory, connotation allows speakers to use a word such as *drop* in any way they please, so long as the linking among domains retains the original sense of the word by associative inference. In practice, however, connotation is constrained by cultural conventions. Thus, while the potential domain of signification for connotative uses of signs is infinite, in practice the extended meanings of signs are often limited by social factors.

4.1.1 Connotative concepts

Path analyses of conversations show, above all else, that discourse is structured largely by connotative inter-network linkages. A truly interesting feature that path analysis also reveals can be called *connotative chaining*. This occurs when a specific connotative node generates derivative associations in the immediate span of the discourse. For instance, once a word such as *drop* is used connotatively by a speaker in a certain situation, then it may spawn a chain of associated concepts such as *pick up, let* go, etc. Here is an example of a discourse excerpt that I recorded at the University of Toronto, during which a speaker (a university student) used the word *drop* as just described:

> Yeah, I *dropped* that course yesterday...No, I won't *pick* it *up* next year...The main reason for *letting it go* was the prof. He was awful...Believe me, I haven't *lost* anything...

In this sample of discourse, the connotative meaning of *drop* initiated a circuit on its own that included *pick up, let go,* and *lose* in close proximity to each other. In effect, the image of 'falling' is distributed in the circuit, surfacing in various lexical forms. The path diagram of this discourse excerpt can be drawn as follows:

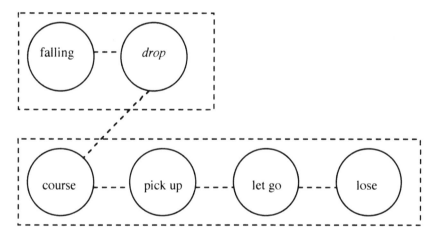

Figure 28. Path analysis of a circuit triggered by *drop*

Note that the nodes are linked again through a process of *association-by-inference—picking up* something means that it was *dropped*; *losing* something elicits the image of *dropping* it; and, of course, *letting* something *go* will cause it to *drop*. The construction of the circuit is a subjective act, based on grafting nodes from network domains. This is what makes discourse unpredictable in actual form, but understandable, and even predictable, conceptually.

Once connotative circuits have been introduced into discourse they tend to guide the flow of conversation through chaining. In the above circuit, for instance, the *pick up* node led a little later in the conversation to the use of *take*, which, in turn, generated its own circuitry with two nodes—*carry* and *heavy*:

> I really can't *take* any more subjects...I'm already *carrying* the maximum...I've got quite a *heavy* load...

The path analysis of the two relevant stretches of conversation shows the following two connotative chains

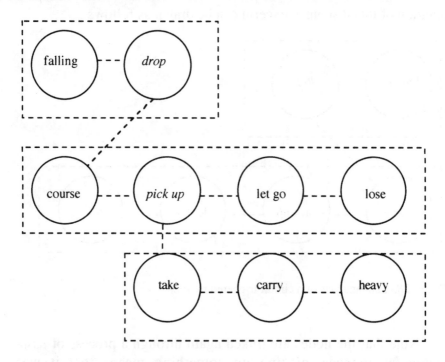

Figure 29. Path analysis of two circuits generated by *drop*

As mentioned in chapter 2, (§2.1.1), the position of the nodes relative to each other in each network and circuit is not relevant—

only the fact that they are connected in specific ways is the relevant feature of network analysis. Indeed, there is no way of realistically charting directionality as it occurs in mind-space. Path diagrams constitute, simply, techniques for showing on paper how conceptual structure is both highly subjective, yet highly understandable.

In generativist theories of language, denotation is considered to be the primary shaper of the cognitive flow of meaning during discourse, and connotation a secondary, context-dependent option within this flow. But this view is not supported by the plethora of findings on discourse in general (e.g. Pollio, Barlow, Fine, and Barlow 1977) nor by path analysis. Michel Foucault (1972) characterized sense-making appropriately as the product of an endless "interrelated fabric" in which the boundaries of meanings are never clear-cut. Every signifier is caught up in a system of references to other signifiers, to codes, and to texts. As soon as one questions that unity, Foucault emphasized, it loses its self-evidence; it indicates itself.

4.1.2 Narrative circuits

There are various kinds of connotative circuits that characterize discourse flow. Some of these contain nodes based on *narrative* traditions; these are concepts referring to themes, plot-lines, characters, and settings that surface in narratives. Calling someone a *Casanova* or a *Don Juan*, rather than *lady-killer*, evokes an array of socially-significant connotations that these characters embody. Referring to a place as *Eden* or *Hell* elicits connotations that have a basis in mythic and religious narrative.

A research project I conducted with students at the University of Lugano in the spring of 1999 revealed that narrative circuits can be found in many connotative networks. The students were asked to jot down all the ideas that certain concepts evoked. They were then asked to join them with the technique of network diagramming. The following partial network, constructed by one student, was evoked by the word *bianco* 'white'. Note that among other nodes in its complex circuitry, one finds nodes referring to Dante's *Divine Comedy*, *Beatrice*, his paramour, and associated nodes such as *paradiso* 'paradise'. These are interconnected with such nodes as *divinità* 'divinity', *spirito* 'spirit', *anima* 'soul', *purezza* 'purity', *candore* 'candor', *neve* 'snow', *freddo* 'cold', *castità* 'chastity', *leggerezza* 'lightness', *volo* 'flight', *cielo* 'sky', *nuvole* 'clouds', *luce* 'light', *Madonna* 'the Madonna', *colore* 'color':

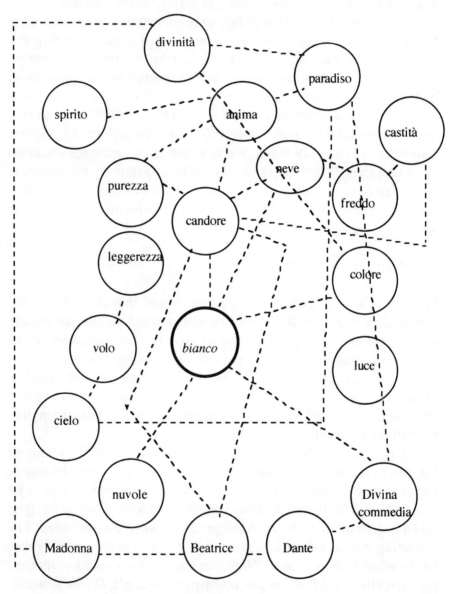

Figure 30.   Connotative network for *bianco*

The student then showed how each one of these nodes leads on its own to other networks and generates offshoot circuitry: e.g. *luce* leads to *illumnazione* 'illumination', to *scoprire (la luce)* 'discover truth', etc. The experiment showed, overall, that the students were able to analyze conceptual domains as systems of knowledge based on connotative circuits, many of which were generated by narrative traditions. The experiment also showed that there is much criss-crossing and looping in connotative networks, corroborating, indirectly, what the scholar Vladimir Propp (1928) claimed —namely that ordinary discourse is built upon an entangled associative connotative structure based in large part on narrative thinking.

This line of inquiry would explain, in effect, why narrative is the medium through which children come to learn values, ethics, morals, etc. Stories of imaginary beings and events allow children to make sense of the world of abstract thinking, providing the intelligible circuits through which they can navigate mentally, thus learning from *association-by-inference*. Such mental navigation imparts the sense that there is a *plot* to life, that the *characters* in it subserve some meaningful purpose, and that the *setting* of life is part of the human condition.

This line of inquiry also suggests two key psychological principles that are especially important when it comes to SLA research:

- Abstract concepts are understood primarily in terms of connotative circuitry.

- The organization of concepts in memory is thus probably associative.

Narrative circuits imbue all kinds of texts with layers and layers of cultural meanings. For example, the surface text of the movie *Blade Runner* unfolds as a science fiction detective story, but its subtext is, arguably, a religious text —the search for a Creator (Danesi and Perron 1999). This textual picture is completed by the many intertextual allusions to Biblical themes and symbols in the movie. Extracting meaning from such narrative texts is thus dependent on the ability to navigate the narrative circuits that undergird the structure of the surface text.

4.1.3 Mythic circuits

The word *myth* derives from the Greek *mythos* 'word', 'speech', 'tale of the gods'. It is a narrative in which the characters are gods, heroes, and mystical beings, the plot is about the origin of things or about dramatic human events influenced by the gods, and the setting is a metaphysical world juxtaposed against the real world. The *mythic circuits* that have been extracted from these stories also surface constantly in common discourse events. Climatologists, for example, refer to the warming of the ocean surface off the western coast of South America that occurs every 4 to 12 years when upwelling of cold, nutrient-rich water does not occur as a person, *El Niño*, 'the little one' in Spanish. This mythic personification of a climatological condition makes it much more understandable in human terms. Although people do not think of *El Niño* as a mythic figure, they nonetheless find it convenient to blame it for certain weather repercussions as if it were one. This is how original myths worked cognitively—the difference being that the personified conditions of the past were actually believed to be real gods or mythical beings. The discourse that surrounds *El Niño* is virtually always interpretable in mythic terms. For instance, I recorded a weather commentary on American television recently that contained a circuit generated by the device of mythic personification:

> This year *El Niño* is having a great time of it. *He* has *wreaked havoc upon* anyone or anything in *his* path. *He* has *come down* very strenuously upon us.

Rarely do we realize how much of the conceptual fabric of modern signifying orders is cut from myth. From the original myths we have inherited, for instance, the names of the days of the week and months of the year: e.g. *Tuesday* is the day dedicated to the Germanic war god Tir; *Wednesday* to the Germanic chief god Wotan, *Thursday* to Thor, *Friday* to the goddess of beauty Frigga, *Saturday* to the god Saturn, *January* to the Roman god Janus, and so on. Our planets bear a similar pattern of nomenclature: *Mars* is named after the Roman god of war, *Venus* after the Greek god of beauty, etc. The residues of mythic thinking can also be seen in the fact that we continue to read horoscopes, implore the gods to help us, cry out against Fortune, and so on.

The great mythic themes of a life journey, of a battle between good and evil, of a descent into an underworld, and so on, find expression in rituals and in common discourse. In early Hollywood westerns, for instance, the mythic theme of good vs. evil manifested itself in various symbolic and expressive ways: e.g. heroes wore white hats and villains black ones. Sports events, too, are perceived as mythological dramas juxtaposing the good (the home team) vs. the bad (the visiting team). The whole fanfare associated with preparing for the "big event", like the Superbowl of American football, has a ritualistic quality to it similar to the pomp and circumstance that ancient armies engaged in before going out to battle and war. Indeed, the whole event is perceived to be a mythic battle. The symbolism of the home team's (army) uniform, the valor and strength of the players (the heroic warriors), and the skill and tactics of the coach (the army general) has a powerful effect on the fans (the two warring nations). The game (the battle) is perceived to unfold in moral terms, as a struggle of Herculean proportions between the forces of good and evil in the universe. Sports figures are exalted as heroes or condemned as villains. This comes out rather conspicuously in discourse about sports events and heroes. Following are statements recorded from American TV broadcasts that show how intrinsic mythic conceptualization is in the domain of sports:

134. The *Forty-Niners* lost the final battle.
135. That quarterback has fallen from his lofty perch, hasn't he?
136. That team is looked upon favorably by the sports gods.
137. That period of hockey was a titanic struggle for the home side.

Some psychologists, such as the Austrian Sigmund Freud (1856-1939), have even used mythic themes as frameworks for talking about the conflicts and dynamics in the unconscious psychic life of individuals. For example, Freud resorted to the myth of *Oedipus* to explain a subconscious sexual desire in a child for the parent of the opposite sex, usually accompanied by hostility to the parent of the same sex. In Greek mythology, Oedipus the King was abandoned at birth and unwittingly killed his father and then married his mother.

4.1.4 Metaphorical circuits

The third main type of connotative circuit in discourse is derived from metaphorical thinking. The topic of metaphorical concepts will be taken up in the next chapter. Here it is simply mentioned as a source of node-formation in connotative networks.

Take, as an example, the *up-down* metaphorical concept that entails the connotative feature 'verticality'. In verbal discourse this feature is a node that is reflexivized in expressions such as the following:

138. I'm feeling *up*.
139. They're feeling *down*.
140. I'm working my way *up* the ladder of success.
141. His status has gone *down* considerably.

This same concept manifests itself in the religious domain, where goodness, spirituality, and heaven are portrayed as *up*, and evil, damnation, and hell as *down* in sermons, theological narratives, religious visual representations, the design of churches, etc. In public building design, too, it can be discerned in the fact that the taller office buildings in a modern city are the ones that indicate which institutions (and individuals) hold social and economic power. In musical composition, higher tones are typically employed to convey a sensation of happiness, lower ones of sadness. During speech, the raising of the hand designates notions of amelioration, betterment, growth, etc., whereas the lowering of the hand designates the opposite notions. In bodily representation and perception, this concept shows up in the common viewpoint that *taller is more attractive/shorter is less attractive*. In mathematical and scientific representational practices its influence can be seen, for instance, in the ways in which graphs are designed—lines that are oriented in an upward direction indicate a growth or an increase of some kind, while those that are slanted in a downward direction indicate a decline or decrease.

These are just some of the ways in which the *up-down* concept is distributed in the pathways of interconnected conceptual networks in a culture. As can be seen, the web of meanings that constitute the signifying order is a highly cohesive and associative one.

4.2 Connotation in discourse

The following brief stretch of conversation between two students, recorded at the University of Toronto in 1999, shows how a metaphorical node, generated by the [people are animals] conceptual metaphor (chapter 2, §2.1.2), became the source of a connotative chain:

Student A: You know, that prof is a real *snake.*

Student B: Ya', I know, he's a real *slippery* guy.

Student A: He somehow always knows how to *slide* around a tough situation when confronted.

Student B: Keep away from his courses; he *bites*!

The connotative circuit can be shown with the following path diagram:

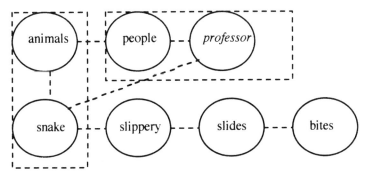

Figure 31. Discourse circuit triggered by [people are animals]

Path analyses, such as this one, show that, not infrequently, a metaphorical concept triggers such connotative chains in terms of a process that may be called *source domain hopping*, because the chain is put together in a way that seems almost as if the speaker is "hopping" from one source domain to another associated with a target concept. In a stretch of conversation based on *ideas*, another student uttered the following sentence:

> I do not *see* how anyone can *swallow* his ideas, especially since most of them have gone *out of fashion*, and thus are *dying* out.

A path analysis of this statement shows that the student re-flexivized the concept of [ideas] in terms of four of its associated source domains — [seeing], [food], [fashion], and [living beings]:

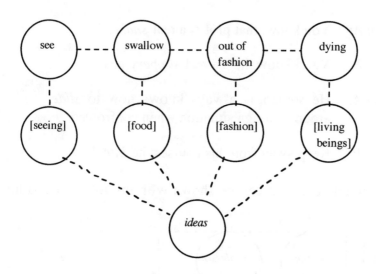

Figure 32.   Discourse circuit triggered by *ideas*

Connotative chaining based on domain hopping is sometimes observable between interlocutors in a conversation. This shows that interlocutors are occasionally influenced by the conceptual structure undergirding a certain conversation. The following dialogue occurred among three colleagues of mine at the University of Toronto in 1999. The relevant parts have been grouped according to speaker. In the actual conversation they occurred at diffe rent points.

> *Speaker A*: I've got to start earning some *bread* by pub-lishing more trendy stuff...I'm practically on a *starvation diet*...No matter how you *slice* it that's the wave of the future in aca-demia.

> *Speaker B*: Hey, you're stepping on a *sacred cow*...But I suppose you're, right, maybe it is time for me too to take the *bull* by the horns.....

> *Speaker C*: You guys are rotten *apples*....You can't *cut* it both ways

The connotative chain initiated by speaker **A** was derived from an association of *money* with *bread*:

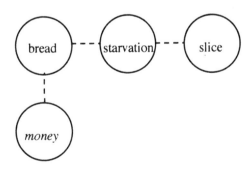

Figure 33. Connotative chain triggered by associating *money* with *bread*

Speaker **B** was influenced by the symbolic religious connota-tions of *bread*, which he associated with scholarly publication. His follow-up statement contains a connotative chain, *sacred cow-bull* that is, in effect, an offshoot circuit:

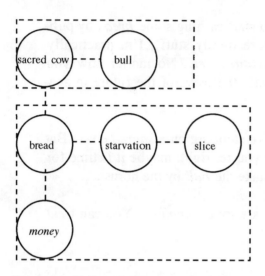

Figure 34. Follow-up discourse circuit interconnected to the *bread* node

Finally, speaker **C**'s circuit is an offshoot of **A**'s *slice* node:

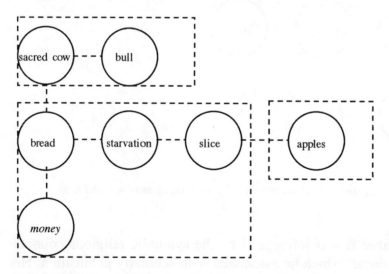

Figure 35. Follow-up discourse circuit interconnected to the *slice* node

The underlying associative structure that interconnects *bread*, *sacred cow* and *apple* is the conceptual metaphor that associates sacredness and knowledge with food symbols. This manifests itself throughout signifying orders. The world's religious ceremonies, for instance, are centered on food symbolism. The *raison d'être* of the Catholic Mass is to partake symbolically of the consecrated body and blood of Christ. Specific types of food are served and eaten traditionally at Thanksgiving, Easter, Christmas, and so on. Food invariably is a primary constituent of all kinds of ceremonies and rituals, from feasts (weddings, anniversaries, etc.) to simple social gatherings. We schedule "breakfast", "lunch", and "dinner" events on a daily basis. Indeed, we plan our days around meals. Even going out on a common date would be virtually unthinkable without some symbolic eating component associated with this courtship ritual (ranging from the popcorn eaten at movie theaters to the elaborate meals consumed at trendy restaurants).

Many of the symbolic meanings of food derive, of course, from mythic and religious accounts of human origins. The story of Adam and Eve in the Western Bible, for instance, revolves around the eating of an apple. In actual fact, the Hebrew account of the Genesis story tells of a *forbidden* fruit, not an *apple*. The representation of this fruit as an apple came in medieval pictorial portrayals of the Eden scene, when painters and sculptors became interested in the Genesis story artistically. In the Koran, on the other hand, the forbidden fruit is a banana. Now, the Biblical symbolism of the apple as *forbidden knowledge* continues to resonate in our culture. This is why the apple tree symbolizes the *tree of knowledge*; why the *Apple* computer company chose the logo of this fruit; why expressions such *the apple of one's eye* abound; and so on. Foods like *bread* and *lamb* also evoke latent religious symbolism in cultures. This is why we talk of the *bread of life*, of *earning your bread*, of *sacrificial lambs*, and the like.

4.2.1 Gesture during discourse

The intuitive feeling that language, gesture, and other nonverbal codes are interconnected can now be made explicit in terms of conceptual structure. Consider, for instance, the interplay between oral discourse and the gesticulation that accompanies it. The research by David McNeill (1992) sheds some truly important light on this interplay. McNeill videotaped a large number of people as they spoke, gathering a vast amount of data on the kinds of gestures that typically accompany speech. McNeill's findings suggest that gestures are complementary components of vocal communication, allowing the speaker to exhibit images that cannot be shown overtly in speech, as well as images of what the speaker is thinking about. Speech and gesture constitute a single integrated communication system in which both cooperate to express the person's intended meanings.

On the basis of his findings, McNeill was able to classify gestures into five main categories. First, there are *iconic* gestures which, as their name suggests, bear a close resemblance to the referent of a concept: e.g. when describing a scene from a story in which a character bends a tree back to the ground, a speaker observed by McNeill appeared to grip something and pull it back. His gesture was, in effect, a visual representation of the action talked about, revealing both his memory image and his point of view (since he could have taken the part of the character or the tree instead).

Second, there are *metaphoric* gestures. These are also pictorial, but their content is abstract. For example, McNeill observed a male speaker announcing that what he had just seen was a cartoon, simultaneously raising up his hands as if offering his listener a kind of object. He was obviously not referring to the cartoon itself, but to the "genre" of the cartoon. His gesture created and displayed this genre as if it were an object, placing it into an act of offering to the listener. This type of gesture typically accompanies utterances that contain metaphorical circuits such as *presenting an idea, putting forth an idea, offering advice*, and so on.

Third, there are *beat* gestures. These resemble the beating of musical tempo. The speaker's hand moves along with the rhythmic pulsation of speech, in the form of a simple flick of the hand or fingers up and down, or back and forth. Beats are used to mark the introduction of new characters, summarize the action, introduce new themes, etc. during the utterance.

Fourth, there are *cohesive* gestures. These serve to show how separate parts of an utterance are supposed to hold together. Beats emphasize sequentiality, cohesives globality. Cohesives can take iconic, metaphoric, or beat form. They unfold through a repetition of the same gesture form, movement, or location in the gesture space. It is the repetition that is meant to convey cohesiveness.

Fifth, there are *deictic* gestures. These are aimed not at an existing physical place, but at an abstract concept that had occurred earlier in the conversation. They reveal that we perceive concepts as having a physical location in space.

McNeill's work gives us a good idea of how the gestural mode of representation intersects with the vocal one in normal discourse. It would seem to be the case that accompanying gestures express an inner need to support what one is saying orally in physical ways. In effect, the various nodes in connotative discourse circuits find expression not only in linear syntax, but also in gestural movements that portray the imagery evoked much more vividly.

4.2.2 Some relevant findings

Network and path analyses of discourse reveal many interesting things about how messages are delivered conceptually, and how certain notions generate complex connotative networks. Several experiments were conducted at the Universities of Toronto, Lugano, and Perugia that bear this out.

In one experiment, the following passage was given to a class of students of Italian at the University if Toronto during the 1998. They were asked to translate it:

> Jack is a real cool cat. He never blows his stack and hardly ever flies off the handle. What's more, he knows how to get away with things. Of course, he is getting on, too. His hair is pepper and salt, but he knows how to make up for lost time by taking it easy. He gets up early, works out, and turns in early.

This passage is rich in connotation and thus poses a truly difficult translation problem, since the true translation must occur at the conceptual, not surface structure, level. A path analysis of this paragraph shows a high degree of crisscrossing, looping, and domain hopping in its conceptual structure:

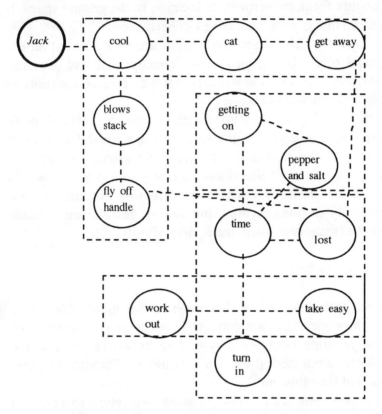

Figure 36. Path diagram of a connotation-rich paragraph

Because of the connotative complexity of the network, at first the students found translation to be an impossible task. So, they were provided with the path diagram above, and then asked to reconfigure it with a conceptual structure that would deliver the same message in Italian. With the help of the instructor and the use of reference materials (dictionaries, phrase books), the students were able to translate it in ways that reflected Italian discourse structure to various degrees of fidelity, as native speakers confirmed by reading and assessing them. One student made the following analogies that allowed her to reconfigure the text in an appropriate manner. In this case, the analogies rendered the text much more denotative, yet still appropriate conceptually:

Table 3. Analogies between English and Italian expressions

English	Italian
to be a (real) cool cat	*essere una persona molto calma*
to blow one's stack	*perdere l'auto-controllo, arrabbiarsi*
to fly off the handle	*arrabbiarsi fortemente*
what's more	*per di più*
to get away with something	*cavarsela*
of course	*certo, naturalmente*
to be getting on	*invecchiarsi*
pepper and salt	*capelli un po' grigi*
to make up for something	*riprendere, riacquistare, rifare*
lost time	*tempo perduto*
to take it easy	*stare calmo, non preoccuparsi*
to get up	*alzarsi dal letto*
to work out	*fare esercizio, fare ginnastica*
to turn in	*andare a dormire la sera*

Each substitution entailed a different reflexivization. This led to the making of several drafts that were edited for grammar and vocabulary. The end result was a composition that delivered the same message as the English one, but in conceptually-appropriate Italian.

Connotative competence consists in an unconscious ability to encode and decode texts in a connotatively-appropriate fashion. One technique for fleshing out the unconscious connotative competence of native-speakers is to ask them to draw up networks of specific concepts. This was the object of a Lugano study in 1998 (above §4.1.2), conducted on 149 students. The same study was repeated several months later with 89 students at the University of Perugia. The students of both universities were asked simply to construct network diagrams of certain concepts.

From the data collected several interesting findings emerged. For instance, the networks constructed for *bianco* (§4.1.2) showed a remarkable consistency. Although there was much variation in the number of circuits, crisscrosses and loops, the conceptual content of nodes was remarkably similar. Of the 238 students that took part in the project, the following nodes were chosen by most (229) in the order of frequency shown:

Table 4. Frequency of nodes in network data collected

Node	Frequency
luce 'light'	97%
purezza 'purity'	91%
pulito 'clean'	87%
neve 'snow'	85%
candore 'candor'	85%
colore 'color'	84%
sposa 'bride'	80%
latte 'milk'	79%
anima 'soul'	77%
verginità 'virginity'	76%
freddo 'cold'	70%

These constitute *primary nodes,* since they are the most common concepts associated with the focal node. Each one of these nodes generated secondary circuits of its own; which were nevertheless fairly productive: e.g. the *luce* node generated the following secondary nodes, shown in order of frequency:

Table 5.   Frequency of the secondary nodes generated by *luce*

Nodes	Frequency
Dio 'God'/ *divinità* 'divinity'	63%
paradiso 'paradise'	62%
illuminato 'enlightened'	58%
Divina commedia	49%
eternità	47%

At the tertiary and later circuit levels, higher and higher degrees of variation showed up. In all, a minimum of 9 and a maximum of 12 levels of noding were recorded with respect to *bianco*: i.e. from 9 to 12 circuits within its network were mapped by the 238 subjects. The following chart shows the consistency level for each one — *consistency* is defined as the average of the percentages for each node. Thus, for instance, the consistency for the primary noding level of *bianco* is computed as the average of the 11 percentages above (97% + 91% + 87% +...70%/11 = 83%). All figures are rounded-off:

Table 6. Consistency levels for the *bianco* concept

Noding level	Number	Consistency
1 (Primary)	211	83%
2 (Secondary)	199	82%
3 (Tertiary)	156	80%
4	98	62%
5	67	56%
6	52	44%
7	45	23%
8	37	12%
9	22	9%
10	8	7%
11	5	1%
12	4	--

This finding suggests that conceptual networks are highly regular and predictable at the primary, secondary, and maybe tertiary levels. Variation occurs mainly at the lower levels. Similar sets of statistics were found for the other concepts used in the project: *cuore* 'heart', *persona* 'person', *oro* 'gold', etc. There were 52 concepts in all. At the primary level of noding the consistencies ranged from 87% to 99%. At the secondary level, they ranged from 34% to 69%.

The project also revealed that certain concepts are more productive than others. Productivity in this framework is defined as the number of nodes and circuits that a certain conceptual network contains. In effect, the more grafting and chaining, the more productive a concept. For example, it was found that *cuore* 'heart' was more productive than *bianco*. It generated 22 circuits, compared to the 12 of *bianco*. Each these circuits then generated many more circuits of their own. Most of the circuits were grafted from highly disparate network domains, producing a high degree of crisscrossing, looping, and hopping.

4.3 Pedagogical considerations

In the fall of 1999, a target language group of second-year students of Italian at the University of Toronto was asked to write compositions on the meaning of *bianco—Cosa significa il bianco per te?* ('What does whiteness mean to you?'). A path analysis of the compositions was then carried out and compared to the networks collected at Lugano and Perugia. It was found that where English and Italian coincided conceptually—e.g. *whiteness* = 'purity', cleanliness', etc.—the compositions could be seen to be appropriate. It was in areas where the two contrasted that the compositions lacked conceptual appropriateness. Circuits initiated by nodes such as *Divina commedia* were completely absent from the Toronto data. Overall, it was found that second-year students had very little knowledge of the associative structure that a connotative concept such as *bianco* evokes in native speakers.

This raises several issues with regard to the development of connotative competence:

- Since connotative circuitry is an intrinsic characteristic of discourse flow, it is obvious that much more pedagogical effort will have to be devoted to developing instructional techniques designed to impart this kind of knowledge to students.

- Emphasis should be put on the primary nodes in conceptual networks, since these are the most productive ones.

- Differences between NL and SL conceptual networks should be examined much more closely in order to derive appropriate pedagogical insights.

- Since connotation is the operative mode in the construction of discourse texts it is obvious that the emphasis in SLT will have to be on this mode, rather than on the denotative one. As we saw in the previous chapter, denotative concepts are formed on the basis of the perceived features that are shared by the members of a referential domain—e.g. 'catness'. In a discourse situation such meanings do indeed surface in a host of situations: e.g. talking about one's cat to someone, describing a cat seen in a pet store, etc. The traditional methods have provided plenty of opportunities for students to decipher and employ denotation in discourse. But they have provided very few opportunities for students to develop the ability to navigate through the connotative circuitry, made up with narrative, mythic, and metaphorical signifieds, that undergirds most of discourse.

In a semiotic approach to SLT, the emphasis would be constantly on showing how grammar and vocabulary reflect underlying conceptual structures. As a concrete example, consider how color terms can be introduced in a classroom situation. Since their main connotative uses are in the area of the emotions, they can be included as part of a unit dealing with emotions. The presentation and treatment of colors should follow a denotative-to-connotative flow of meaning:

Table 7. Teaching color terms

Color terms	NL equivalents	Connotative uses	NL equivalents
arancione	orange	--	--
azzurro	blue	*il Principe azzurro*	Prince Charming
bianco	white	*notte bianca*	sleepless night
colore	color	*tutti i colori*	lot of trouble
giallo	yellow	*giallo dalla rabbia*	extremely angry
grigio	gray	*vita grigia*	dull life
marrone	brown	*fare un marrone*	make a big mistake
nero	black	*umore nero*	dark mood
rosa	pink	*acqua di rosa*	superficiality
rosso	red	*diventare rosso/a*	become embarrassed
verde	green	*al verde*	(financially) broke
viola	violet, purple	--	--

The next step in the pedagogical process would be to show how the color concepts form networks and circuits. For example, the metaphorical node associated with the [emotion is a color] concept is the basis of expressions such as the following in English:

142. He's *green* with envy.
143. She's *red* with anger.

Now, (142) can be seen as the generating source node in a circuit such as the following one:

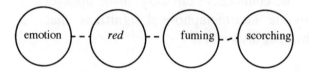

Figure 37. Circuit generated by *red*

This surfaces in such statements as:

144. I'm *fuming*.
145. I'm *scorching* mad.

In Italian it is the *giallo* node that generates a corresponding circuit:

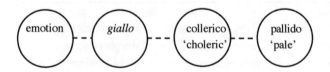

Figure 38. Circuit generated by *giallo*

This surfaces in such statements as:

146. *Non andare in collera* ('Dont' get so angry').
147. *Sono diventato pallido dalla rabbia* ('I became pale with anger').

Such network analyses suggest using traditional pedagogical techniques but gearing them more towards the connotative mode, as the following simple exercise shows:

Fill-in the blanks with appropriate color terms:

Role A   *Anche tu sei di umore _____ (nero)?*
          ('Are you in a dour mood too'?)

Role B   *Eh, sì! Sono quasi sempre al _____ (verde) e faccio una vita _____ (grigia). E tu cos'hai?*
          ('Oh yes! I'm always broke and I live a dull life. What's with you?')

Role A   *Niente. Ultimamente, mia sorella ne sta facendo di tutti i _____ (colori)! Ieri mi ha fatto passare una notte _____(bianca)! E stata quasi tutta la notte al telefono con il suo Principe _____ (azzurro). Mi fa diventare _____ (giallo) dalla rabbia!*
          ('Nothing. Lately my sister has been causing a lot of trouble. Yesterday she made me go through a sleepless night! She was on the phone with her Prince Charming through the night. She makes me red with anger'!)

Students can then be asked to change the connotative effect of certain colors in the above dialogue by utilizing appropriate circuitry. For instance, the last sentence in the dialogue can be changed in several ways to make it more forceful using the nodes shown in figure 38 above:

148. *Mi fa diventare collerico!*
149. *Mi fa diventare pallido dalla rabbia!*

The use of color to refer to emotions can then be used as the basis to teach other concepts by association. For example, the English expression *I'm red in the face* suggests investigating the *face* pedagogically as a source of further connotation:

150. We argued *face* to *face*.
151. Don't show your *face* on my property again.
152. He criticized the supervisor to her *face*.
153. Put on a happy *face*.
154. You wear your feelings on your *face*.
155. You can see his hypocrisy on his *face*.
156. He's just another pretty *face*.
157. I have no *face* for it.

Now, the relevant pedagogical questions to a teacher of Italian are: Is *faccia* used for the same associative reason? If so, in which ways is its use similar and in which ways is it different? As it turns out the connotative signifieds of Italian *faccia* are isomorphic, overlapping, and differentiated, as can be seen from the following examples:

158. *Ha una faccia tosta* ('He is impudent').
159. *Ha la faccia pulita* ('He is honest').
160. *Ha cambiato faccia* ('He did an about face').
161. *Ha una faccia lunga* (He has a long face').
162. *Ha due facce* ('He has two personalities').
163. *Gli ho letto in faccia* ('I read his face').

Once students have discovered the similarities and differences, they can be involved in traditional pattern practice, translation, roleplaying, and other such activities. In effect, imparting connotative competence is not much different than imparting denotative competence. It will just take more time and effort to do so.

Chapter V
Metaphorical concepts

5. Introductory remarks

As discussed several times in the previous chapter, metaphor is often the source of connotative circuitry in discourse. The purpose of this final chapter is to complete the discussion of metaphor by dealing directly with it in an applied semiotic framework.

With few exceptions—notably Giambattista Vico (1688-1744) and Friedrich Nietzsche (1844-1900)—metaphor has not been viewed traditionally in philosophy and psychology as an intrinsic component of language and discourse. It has been considered typically to be a stylistic option for sprucing up literal ways of speaking. However, in the twentieth century, from extensive research in semiotics, Gestalt psychology, pragmatic philosophy, and cognitive linguistics (e.g. Allwood and Gärdenfors 1998; Dirven and Verspoor 1998), it has become obvious that metaphor is not only a regular inbuilt feature of language, but also the source of many abstract concepts and cultural symbolism. For example, referring to *time* can only be accomplished through the template of metaphor, even though this is hardly ever recognized. Consider the following statements:

164. That job *cost* me an hour.
165. He's *wasting* my time.
166. That's not *worth* the time or the effort.
167. *Put aside* some time for her too.

The use of *cost* in (164) is motivated by a general metaphorical concept that has the form [time is money]; the use of *waste* in (165) and *worth* in (166) is traceable to the concept [time is a valuable commodity]; and the use of *put aside* in (167) to [time is an object]. Many of the grammatical forms and categories that are used in surface discourse are, in fact, connectable to such underlying conceptual structures. As we saw in chapter 1 (§1.4.1), Lakoff and Johnson (1980) call these *conceptual metaphors*.

Studies of student discourse show that lack of knowledge of SL conceptual metaphors is at the root of much of the "unnaturalness" that characterizes their speech and the source of most of the errors in their interlanguages (Danesi 1993a, 1993b; Russo 1997). As mentioned throughout this book, this is due in large part to the fact that students have had little or no opportunity to access metaphor network domains and the circuits that they generate in discourse.

5.1 Metaphor

The work on metaphor in anthropology and linguistics over the past three decades (e.g. Dundes 1972; Beck 1982; Lakoff and Johnson 1980, 1999; Kövecses 1986, 1988, 1990; Lakoff 1987; Johnson 1987) has discarded, once and for all, the notion that metaphor is a simple stylistic option to literal language. As a source of network structures, it can be approached pedagogically in ways that that have already been discussed in previous chapters vis-à-vis denotative and connotative concepts. Like connotation, metaphor is the result of a process that has been called previously *association-by-inference*.

Since the psychological notion of *association* has been employed as the central feature of network theory, it is necessary to digress briefly here in order to elucidate what is intended by this term. In psychology, *associationism* is the theory that the mind learns by combining simple, irreducible elements through mental connection. Aristotle (384-322 BC) recognized four strategies by which associations are forged: (1) through *similarity* (e.g. an orange and a lemon), (2) through *difference* (e.g. hot and cold), (3) through *contiguity* in time (e.g. sunrise and a rooster's crow), and (4) through *contiguity* in space (e.g. a cup and saucer). British empiricist philosophers John Locke (1632-1704) and David Hume (1711-1776) saw sensory perception as the underlying factor in such processes. In the nineteenth century, the Aristotelian view was examined empirically, leading eventually to the foundation of an associationist school of psychology, guided by the principles enunciated by James Mill (1773-1836) in his *Analysis of the Phenomena of the Human Mind* (1829). In addition to Aristotle's original four strategies, the school found that such factors as *intensity*, *inseparability*, and *repetition* added to the strength of an association: e.g. *arms* are associated with *bodies* because they are inseparable from them; *rainbows* are associated with *rain* because of repeated observations of the two co-occurring; etc.

The one who developed associationism experimentally was Edward Thorndike (1874-1949), who extended the work initiated by the Russian psychologist Ivan Pavlov (1849-1936) in 1904. Pavlov provided an empirical basis for investigating how associations through repetition are made. When Pavlov presented a meat stimulus to a hungry dog, for instance, the animal would salivate spontaneously, as expected. This was the dog's "unconditioned response". After Pavlov rang a bell while presenting the meat stimulus a number of times, he found that the dog would eventually salivate only to the ringing bell, without the meat stimulus. Clearly, Pavlov suggested, the ringing by itself, which would not have triggered the salivation initially, had brought about a "conditioned response" in the dog. By *association* the dog had learned something new. Every major behavioral psychologist has utilized the Pavlovian notion of associationism. Although behaviorists believe all thought processes can be accounted for through associations of stimuli and responses, other psychologists strongly reject such an approach as inadequate to explain creative thought and verbal behavior.

The meaning of *association* as used in this book is not the Pavlovian one. In line with nineteenth century associationists and twentieth century Gestalt psychologists, it is used here to stress that signs beget their meanings only in relation to other signs. The relations can be forged by sense, i.e. by observing physical features of referents, or by inference, i.e. by applying the sense associations to referents that are perceived as possessing the same features.

Although interest in metaphor was kindled by Aristotle, the scientific study of its relation to concept-formation and discourse is a relatively recent phenomenon. Aristotle was, in fact, the one who coined the term *metaphor*—itself a metaphor (*meta* 'beyond' + *pherein* 'to carry')—pointing out that many abstract forms of knowledge are grounded in associative metaphorical reasoning. However, Aristotle also affirmed that, as knowledge-productive as it was, the most common function of metaphor was to decorate literal ways of thinking and speaking. Remarkably, this latter assertion was the one that was embraced by most Western philosophers. But nothing could be farther from the truth. In 1977, the research team of Pollio, Barlow, Fine, and Pollio conducted an extensive investigation of common discourse texts and found them to be immersed in metaphorical reasoning. They found that speakers of English, for instance, uttered on average 3,000 novel metaphors and 7,000 idioms per week. Obviously, they remarked, metaphor can hardly be considered an ornamental option to literal language.

5.1.1 Conceptual vs. specific metaphors

As mentioned above, concepts such as [time is money] are called *conceptual metaphors*; their specific instantiations in actual discourse are called *specific metaphors*. For example, the expression *Danny is a snake* is a specific instantiation of the [people are animals] conceptual metaphor. This concept is the reason why we also refer to people as *gorillas, snakes, pigs, puppies,* and so on. Each of the two parts of a conceptual metaphor is called a *domain* (chapter 2, §2.1.2): [humans] is the *target domain* [animals] the *source domain*.

The meanings that emerge from the assemblage of source domain vehicles with the target domain concept are connotative. Take again the example *Danny is a snake*. The meaning of *snake* that this statement is designed to convey is not its denotative one, but rather, the culture-specific connotations perceived in snakes. Each different node in this circuit changes the connotative view we get of the topic: e.g. in *Danny is a rat*, *Danny* is portrayed instead as someone *aggressive, combative, rude,* etc.—a circuit of connotative meanings that is generated by the node *rat*.

As these examples show, metaphorical networks constitute conceptual strategies for understanding abstract notions such as *slyness, betrayal, aggressiveness, kindness,* etc. Each different selection of a node from a circuit—*snake, rat, gorilla, pussycat, hog,* etc.—provides a different strategy for depicting specific personalities. Thus, for instance, the specific utilization of the *snake* node generates a circuit with nodes that are types of snakes, allowing one to zero in on specific details of the personality being described:

168. He's a *cobra*.
169. She's a *viper*.
170. Your friend is a *boa constrictor*.

Such metaphors pervade common discourse, as Pollio and his associates showed so convincingly. A few examples will suffice to make this evident.

[happiness is up]/[sadness is down]

171. Today she's feeling *up*.
172. Generally she feels *down*.
173. His comment *boosted* my spirits.
174. My mood *sank* after she told me what happened.
175. His joke gave me a *lift*.

[health and life are up]/[sickness and death are down]

176. Everyone in my family is at the *peak* of health.
177. Unfortunately, my cousin *fell* ill.
178. My job is an *uphill* struggle.
179. Lazarus *rose* from the dead.
180. They're *sinking* fast.

[light is knowledge]/[dark is ignorance]

181. The whole class was *illuminated* by that professor.
182. I was left in the *dark* about what happened.
183. Her explanation is very *clear*.
184. Quantum theory is *obscure*.
185. His example *shed light* on several matters.

[theories are buildings]

186. Hers is a *well-constructed* theory.
187. His theory too is on solid *ground*.
188. But that theory needs more *support*.
189. Otherwise the theory will *collapse* under criticism.
190. Alexander put together the *framework* of a very interesting theory.

[ideas and theories are plants]

191. My professor's ideas have come to *fruition* very late.
192. That's a *budding* theory.
193. Plato's ideas have contemporary *offshoots*.
194. That idea has become a *branch* of mathematics.

[ideas are commodities]

195. My friend certainly knows how to *package* his ideas.
196. However, that idea just won't *sell*.
197. There's no *market* for that idea.
198. That's a *worthless* idea.

As Lakoff and Johnson emphasize, we do not detect the presence of metaphor in such common expressions because of repeated usage. We no longer interpret the word *see* in sentences such as *I don't see what you mean; Do you see what I'm saying?* in metaphorical terms, for instance, because its use in such expressions has become so familiar to us. But the association between the biological act of seeing outside the body with the imaginary act of seeing within the mind was originally the source of the conceptual metaphor [understanding is seeing] which now permeates common discourse:

199. There is more to this than *meets the eye*.
200. I have a different *point of view*.
201. It all depends on how you *look* at it.

202. I take a *dim view* of the whole matter.
203. I never *see eye to eye* on things with you.
204. You have a different *worldview* than I do.
205. Your ideas have given me great *insight* into life.

Note that a target domain can be associated with several source domains: e.g. [ideas] is associated with [buildings] (examples 186-190), [plants] (examples 191-194), and [commodities] (examples 195-198):

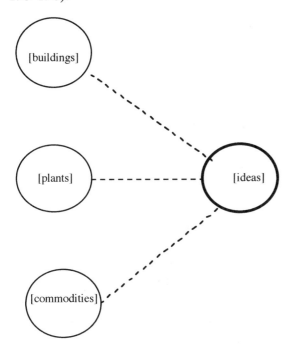

Figure 39. Source domains for *ideas*

As we saw in the previous chapter, such multiple associations constitute the source of domain hopping in discourse (Chapter 4, §4.2). Notice, as well, that different target domains may be associated with the same source domains: e.g. both [time] (examples 165-166) and [ideas] (examples 195-198) are associated with the [commodities] source domain. This is often the source of connotative chaining (chapter 4, §4.1.1):

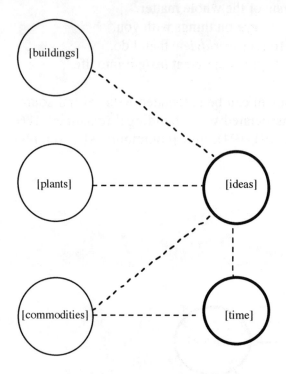

Figure 40. A metaphorical network linking *ideas* and *time*

This explains why we often chain together certain concepts in discourse. For example, *time* and *ideas* can be coupled in sentences— e.g. *That idea isn't worth a second of my time*—and in discourses through the circuit because they are grafted from the circuit containing the common [commodities] node.

Now, the selection of specific vehicles from a source domain becomes, in effect, a potential generating circuit in discourse. Consider the conceptual metaphor [argument is war]. The target domain of [argument] is conceptualized in terms of warlike activities (the source domain). These then influence the actual perception of arguments as unfolding in terms of battles that can be won or lost, of positions that can be attacked or guarded, of ground that can be gained or lost, of lines of attack that can be abandoned or defended, and so on, This chain of associations can be shown as a network of interconnected circuits as follows:

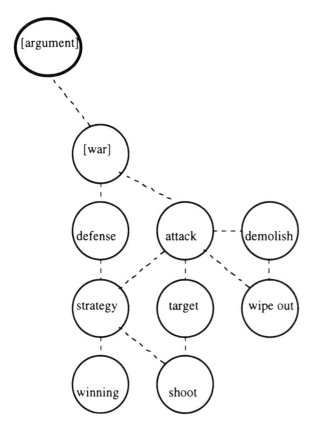

Figure 41. Partial network generated by the [argument is war] concept

This kind of circuitry underlies surface statements such as the following:

206. Your claims are *indefensible.*
207. You *attacked* all my weak points.
208. Your criticisms were *right on target.*
209. I *demolished* his argument.
210. I've never *won* an argument.
211. She *shot down* all my points.
212. If you use that *strategy,* I'll *wipe you out.*

5.1.2 Image schemas

According to Lakoff and Johnson there are three general kinds of associative processes involved in the formation of conceptual metaphors. The first one involves mental *orientation*. This produces concepts that are derived from our physical experiences of *up vs. down, back vs. front, near vs. far*, etc. For example, the experience of *up vs. down* underlies such expressions as:

213.   I'm feeling *up* today (a specific instantiation of [happiness is up]).

214.   She's feeling *down* today (a specific instantiation of [sadness is down]).

215.   My income went *up* last year (a specific instantiation of [more is up]).

216.   Her salary went *down* when she changed jobs (a specific instantiation of [less is down]).

The second type involves *ontological* thinking. This produces conceptual metaphors in which activities, emotions, ideas, etc. are associated with entities and substances: e.g. [the mind is a container]. Again, common discourse is replete with specific metaphors generated by such thinking:

[life is a container]

217.   Student life is *full* of work.
218.   My life is *teeming* with happy memories.
219.   My life is *spilling over* with things to do.

[the mind is a container]

220.   My memory is *empty*.
221.   Put this idea *into* your mind, right away.

222. I can't quite get her *out of* my mind.

[time is an entity, substance, or object]

223. I've *thrown away* too much time.
224. This is *eating up* too much time.
225. I haven't *had too much* time on my hands lately.

The third type of process consists in a mental elaboration of the other two. This produces *structural metaphors* that distend orientational and ontological concepts:

226. His argument *demolished* me (is an instantiation of [argument] as both [war] and [living being]).

227. Lack of time is *destroying* me (is an instantiation of [time] as both [war] and [living being]).

Lakoff and Johnson refer to *image schemas* (Lakoff and Johnson 1980; Lakoff 1987; Johnson 1987) as the psychological sources of such associative processes, defining them as largely unconscious mental outlines of recurrent shapes, actions, dimensions, activities, etc. that derive from perception and sensation and which allow us to visualize abstract notions as concrete things. Image schemas are so deeply rooted that we are hardly ever aware of their control over conceptualization. But they can always be conjured up easily. If someone were to be asked to explain an idiom such as *spill the beans*, in terms of questions such as, "Where were the beans before they were spilled"? "How big was the container"? "Was the spilling on purpose or accidental"? etc., then the person would no doubt start to visualize the appropriate schema of the beans as being kept in a [container]; about the size of the human head; etc.

Image schemas are evidence of "abstractive seeing" as the philosopher Susanne Langer (1948) so aptly put it. As an example, consider the image schema called an [impediment]. This is essentially a mental outline of an obstacle:

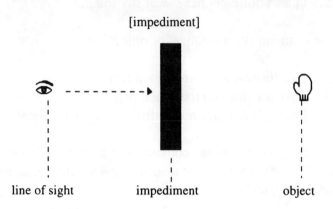

Figure 42. The [impediment] image schema

Several abstract scenarios are now imaginable in terms of this schema: one can go around the impediment, go over it, under it, through it, or remove it and continue on towards the object. On the other hand, the impediment could successfully impede someone, so that one would stop at the impediment and turn back. These scenarios constitute the reason why we say such things as:

228.   We *got through* that difficult time.
229.   Jim felt better after he *got over* his cold.
230.   You want to *steer clear* of financial debt.
231.   With the bulk of the work *out of the way*, he was able to call it a day.
232.   The rain *stopped us* from enjoying our picnic.
233.   You cannot *go any further* with that idea; you'll just have to *turn back*.

I would like to suggest that image schema theory can be expanded to include other kinds of mental imagistic processes. Schemas can also be elicited by fictitious (a *winged table*) or narrative events through which episodes are recalled. Images can also be elicited by various sensory modalities. The following referents can in fact be "heard", "smelled", "touched", etc. in mind-space: (1) the sound of thunder, (2) the feel of wet grass, (3) the smell of fish, (4) the taste of toothpaste, (5) the sensation of being uncomfortably cold, (6) the sensation of extreme happiness.

5.1.3 Cognitive models

Lakoff and Johnson assert that a large portion of cultural groupthink is built on conceptual metaphors. This is accomplished by a kind of "higher-order" metaphorizing. As target domains are associated with many kinds of source domains, the concepts become increasingly more complex, leading to what they call *cultural* or *cognitive models*. To see what this means, consider the network domain of *sports talk*. The following source domains, among many others, underlie a large portion of discourse circuits that characterize such talk:

[fortune]

234.   That team is *lucky*.
235.   Their victory was *unpredictable*.

[war]

236.   They were soundly *defeated*.
237.   That team has a good *attack* but a poor *defense*.

[game-playing]

238.   That was a great *move*.
239.   That team's strategy is *illogical*.

[economics]

240.   That team *earned* a hard-fought tie.
241.   That team's *worth* is going up constantly.

[eating]

242.   That team is *hungry* for a victory.

243. They lose all the time because they are not *thirsty* for victory.

[thought system]

244. Their *approach* to the game is excellent.
245. They now have a winning *mentality*.

The constant circuitry that such source domains generate in common discourse networks produces, cumulatively, a *cognitive model* of sports. This is, in effect, a complex network in which various source domains are associated with the same target domain.

5.1.4 Metonymy and irony

Before Lakoff and Johnson's trend-setting work, the study of metaphor fell within the field of *rhetoric*, where it was viewed as one of various *tropes*—i.e. figures of speech. But since the mid-1905s the practice has been to use the term *metaphor* to refer to the study of all figurative language and to consider the other tropes as particular kinds of metaphor. Within this framework, *personification*, for instance (*My cat speaks Chinese*), would be seen as a particular kind of metaphor, one in which the target domain is an animal or inanimate object and the source domain a set of vehicles that are normally associated with human beings (the paradigmatic opposite of the [people are animals] concept).

But there two tropes that are regularly considered separately from metaphor—metonymy and irony. *Metonymy* entails the use of an entity to refer to another that is related to it:

246. He likes *Bronte* (= the writings of Bronte).
247. My mom hates *nose rings* (= the fact that I am wearing them).
248. The *automobile* is destroying health (= the collection of automobiles).
249. How many *faces* are there in the audience (= people).

250. I bought a *Saturn* (= car named *Saturn*).
251. The *buses* are on strike (= bus drivers).
252. The *White House* was silent about the incident (= the president, the American government).

In parallelism with the notion of *conceptual metaphor*, *conceptual metonym* can be suggested as the underlying conceptual form for such utterances. For instance, the conceptual metonym underlying the following sentences is [the face stands for the person]:

253. He's just another pretty *face*.
254. There are an awful lot of new *faces* in that movie.
255. There are too many familiar *faces* around here.

Conceptual metonyms, like conceptual metaphors, are interconnected to other domains of signification in a culture. The concept [the face stands for the person] is the reason why portraits, in painting and photography, focus on the face. The face is, in effect, a metonym for personality. Here are some other examples of conceptual metonyms:

[the part stands for the whole]

256. Get your *butt* over here!
257. The Blue Jays need a *stronger arm* in right field.
258. We don't hire *crew cuts*.

[the producer stands for the product]

259. I'll have a *Heineken*.
260. We bought a *Ford*.
261. He's got a *Rembrandt* in his office.

[the object used stands for the user]

262. My *piano* is sick today.

263.   The *meat and potatoes* is a lousy tipper.
264.   The *buses* are on strike.

[the institution stands for the people behind it]

265.   *Shell* has raised its prices again.
266.   The *Church* thinks that promiscuity is immoral.
267.   I don't approve of *Washington's* actions.

[the place stands for the institution]

268.   The *White House* isn't saying anything.
269.   *Milan* is introducing new jackets this year.
270.   *Wall Street* is in a panic.

Irony is the use of words to convey a contrary meaning—e.g. *I love being tortured*. It is a verbal strategy that allows an addresser to make a comment on a situation without any personal stake or involvement in it. As such, it is both a protective strategy, deflecting attention away from the Self towards others by which one can make value judgments of others without commitment, and a verbal weapon that can be used aggressively towards others. Irony produces what Hutcheon (1995) calls various degrees of an "affective charge" (i.e. emotional involvement). In terms of network theory, ironic statements can be seen to result when nodes delivering a paradigmatically-opposite meaning are interconnected. This hopping across network domains to make ironic associations generates unexpected circuitry: e.g. *torture* and *love* are not part of the same networks. However, once associated they generate circuits of their own:

271.   I love being tortured.
272.   She loves getting hurt.
273.   He enjoys torment.

Both metonymy and irony can however be treated pedagogically under the same rubric. The main point to be made here is that knowing how these constitute conceptual fluency will put SLT into a better position to incorporate them into instructional practices and into the development of appropriate pedagogical materials.

5.2 Metaphorical circuits

In the semiotic framework adopted in this book, a specific metaphorical concept is construable as a node in conceptual networks. Some of these, as we have seen above, are sources for derived metaphorical circuitry. Once the primary circuits have been formed, on the basis of associations between target and source domains, then each node in such circuits becomes a new productive source for creating secondary circuits; and these become sources for tertiary circuits; and so on.

5.2.1 Primary circuits

The conceptual metaphor [thinking is seeing], which results from an association between [thinking] and [seeing] domains generates a primary circuit made up of such nodes as *seeing*, *visualizing*, etc.

274. I cannot *see* what possible use your idea might have.
275. I cannot quite *visualize* what that theory is all about.
276. That idea has given me great *insight* into human nature.

Primary circuits are the ones that most native speakers recognize instantly as the conceptual material for instantiating a specific conceptual metaphor. The circuitry underlying the above statements can be represented as follows:

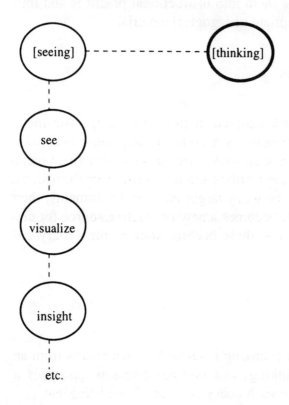

Figure 43. Circuit generated by [thinking is seeing]

Another source domain for [thinking] is that of [geometrical figures/relations]:

277. Those ideas are *circular*.
278. I don't see the *point* of your idea.
279. Her ideas are *central* to the discussion.
280. Their ideas are *diametrically* opposite.

The two connected circuits form a network to which other derived or related circuits can be added. The fragment of the network formed by the above two can be represented as follows:

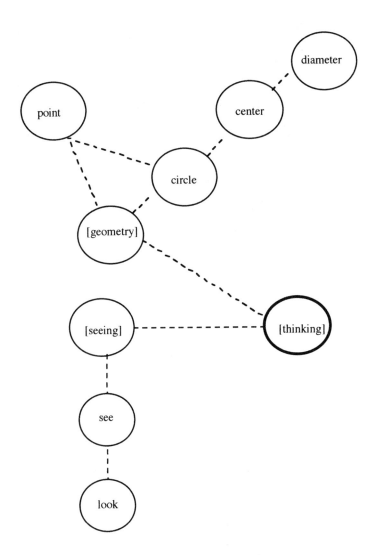

Figure 44. Partial network for [thinking is seeing]

A network such as the one above is characterized by the presence of different source domain nodes interconnected to the same
target node. All cognitive models are networks of this type.

5.2.2 Secondary circuits

As Haden Elgin (2000: 90), puts it: "One of the characteristics of metaphor that gets far too little attention is that metaphors don't stand alone—they bring other metaphors with them". This describes rather accurately the notion of secondary circuit. In the circuit generated by [seeing] in the [thinking is seeing] network above (§5.2.1) the *look* node is the source of a circuit made up of nodes such as *up, over, through,* etc.:

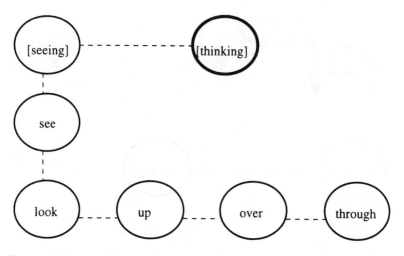

Figure 45. Secondary metaphorical circuit

This secondary circuit is the source of statements such as:

281. Where did you *think up* that idea?
282. I *thought over* carefully your ideas.
283. You should *think through* the whole problem.

The intricate networks that primary and secondary circuits form produce higher-order abstractions. The greater the density of the circuitry, the more abstract and, thus, more culture-specific, the conceptual network. Primary circuitry generated by the [thinking is seeing] conceptual metaphor is relatively understandable across cultures: i.e. people from non-English-speaking cultures could easily figure out what the statements that instantiate this metaphor mean if they were translated to them, because they connect a concrete source domain—e.g. *seeing*—to an abstraction—*thinking*—directly. Secondary circuitry on the other hand, is more likely to be understood primarily in culture-specific ways, and thus the statements that instantiate such circuitry are much harder to translate, because they connect concrete (primary) metaphorical vehicles to further abstractions. Thus, expressions such as *I see your point, I can't visualize what you're saying* have equivalents in Italian. But expressions such as *think up* and *think over* do not, and are much harder to render in Italian.

5.2.3 Tertiary circuits

Tertiary circuits are generated by secondary nodes. The [thinking is seeing] network above (§5.2.1) also generates a secondary circuit from the *seeing* node based on the fact that seeing occurs in the *light*:

284. That theory shed *light* on many matters.
285. I have been left in the *dark* about the affair.
286. That is a truly *bright* idea.

This circuit can be represented as follows:

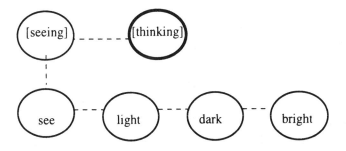

Figure 46. Secondary metaphorical circuit

Now, the *light* node in this circuit can generate such derived concepts as *chiaroscuro, illumination, visionary,* etc. that are obviously associated metaphorically with *light*:

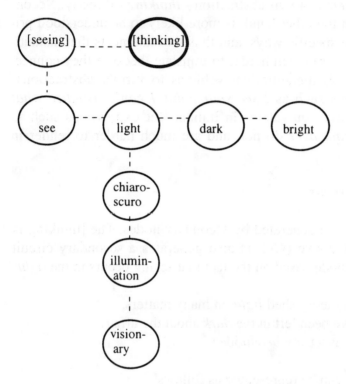

Figure 47. Tertiary metaphorical circuit generated by the *light* node

These concepts are, needless to say, much more tied to a signifying order and thus not easily translatable. The art of *chiaroscuro*—the technique of using light and shade in painting, invented by the Italian baroque painter Michelangelo Merisi da Caravaggio (1573-1610)—is in fact an Italian word that was simply *borrowed* in English. The *light* node is also the source for the portrayal of *illumination* and *visionary* experiences in terms of dazzling sensations of light. Needless to say, tertiary nodes can themselves be the source of subsequent circuitry. For example, a *rose* is used as a symbol for *love* in Western culture because it derives ultimately from the metaphorical association of *love* to a *sweet smell*, to the color *red*, and to the notion that love grows like a *plant*—all nodes in spin-off circuits in the network for *love*.

The foregoing analysis of metaphorical networks is intended to show how highly interconnected abstractions are to each other and how they are utilized to generate conceptual structures and systems. These networks are also interconnected with nonverbal systems of representation. The [people are animals] network is the source of such symbolic activities as the use of animals in totemic codes, in heraldic traditions, in the creation of fictional characters for use in story-telling to children *(Bugs Bunny, Foghorn Leghorn, Daffy Duck*, etc.), in the naming of sports teams (Chicago *Bears*, St. Louis *Cardinals*, Miami *Dolphins*, etc.), and in the creation of surnames, to mention but a few.

Such networks are also found in scientific reasoning. Science often involves things that cannot be seen—atoms, waves, gravitational forces, magnetic fields, etc. So, scientists use their metaphorical know-how to get a look, so to speak, at this hidden matter. That is why waves are said to *undulate* through empty space like water waves ripple through a still pond; atoms to *leap* from one quantum state to another; electrons to *travel in circles* around an atomic nucleus; and so on. The poet and the scientist alike use metaphor to extrapolate a suspected inner connection among things. As physicist Robert Jones (1982: 4) aptly puts it, for the scientist metaphor serves as "an evocation of the inner connection among things". Needless to say, *network theory* is also the product of metaphorical reasoning. Like any theory it is an attempt to *show* what some concept entails—no more, no less.

5.3 Pedagogical considerations

Interest in metaphor and the other tropes in the context of SLA research has been minimal (e.g. Cameron and Low 1999). Within mainstream SLT only one movement, called the *contrastive rhetoric movement*, that was begun in 1966 by Robert Kaplan, can be seen to have some of the same ideas discussed in this book. The key finding of this movement (Kaplan 1978; Kroll 1990; Leki 1991; Connor 1996) is that negative transfer occurs on a discourse level rather than on a lexical or syntactic level. As we have seen in this book, this is due to the fact that the conceptual structure that underlies discourse is largely connotative and metaphorical and thus culture-specific. But, as several pilot projects have shown (Danesi 1992; Russo 1997), this kind of competence—which has been called *semiotic competence* in this book—is as teachable as linguistic or communicative competence, especially if the grammatical system of the SL is viewed as a system encoding the underlying conceptual system.

Research conducted previously on university students of Italian (Danesi 1992, 1993a; Russo 1997) suggests that typical classroom learners show virtually no traces of conceptual fluency, even after several years of study. The reason for this is not that they are incapable of learning SL metaphorical meanings, but more likely that they have never been exposed in formal ways to the conceptual system of the target language and culture. To be conceptually fluent in the SL the student must be able to convert common experiences into conceptually and linguistically appropriate models. At the present time there seems to be very little in SL methodology that takes this into account.

The notions of networks and circuits is intended to make the pedagogical task of imparting conceptual fluency a practicable one. These are not to be construed as "instructions" for generating discourse—like the instructions used in computer programs. Rather, they are intended to show how concepts are interconnected to each other. Conceptual interconnections involve crisscrossing, looping, hopping across denotative, connotative, and metaphorical network. The central goal of pedagogy should be to teach and explain the networks themselves, leaving the task of implementing them up to the students.

The main implications that this basic view of pedagogy entails, as discussed in previous chapters, are the following:

- The primary task facing SL learners is that of conceptual reorganization. This means that they will have to reorganize the signifier-signified relation in the SL whenever it overlaps with, or is differentiated from, the NL relation in the same domain of reference.

- The secondary task facing SL learners is that of learning how to navigate the conceptual networks that underlie discourse. This means that they will have to be able to expand the signifier-signified relation to encompass connotative and metaphorical meanings and to understand how this expansion creates associative networks of meanings.

This view does not imply a radical change in instruction; rather, it entails basically a refocusing of traditional methods and techniques. During a graduate summer course I gave to high school teachers of Italian at Middlebury College in the summer of 1996, I found that conceptual fluency was a notion that could easily be converted into practice. The student-teachers were taught the basic elements of network analysis and then asked to prepare a unit on either *love* or *birthdays* based upon it.

The first thing that they were required to do was to write dialogues. One student wrote a dialogue on birthdays that was structured conceptually by the network based on the conceptual metaphor [age is a quantity]. This underlies expressions in native-speaker discourse such as the following:

287. *Li porti bene gli anni.*
      (literally 'You carry your years well').

288. *Gli anni incominciano a pesare sulle mie spalle.*
      (literally 'The years are beginning to weigh on my shoulders').

289. *Quanti anni hai? Ne ho 22.*
      (literally 'How many years do you have? I have 22 of them').

The dialogue was then evaluated by 3 native speakers (professors from Italy visiting Middlebury College that summer) and found to be "authentic" when compared to those found typically in textbooks. Here is an excerpt from her dialogue:

Role A   *Ciao, Marco, Ho sentito che oggi compi gli anni?*
('Hi Mark, I heard it's your birthday today').

Role B   *Eh, già.*
('That's right').

Role A   *Quanti ne hai?*
('How old are you?').

Role B   *Troppi! Oggi ne faccio 35.*
('Much too old. I'm 35 years old today').

Role A   *Ma, li porti veramente bene.*
('You wouldn't be able to tell').

The student-teachers were then asked to prepare explanatory, grammatical, and activity sections, following up on the dialogue-writing exercise. The quality of their work also demonstrated the facility with which conceptually appropriate practical material could be devised. The student-teacher who composed the above dialogue explained the verbs *portare* and *compiere*, the noun *anni*, and particle *ne* as surface structures resulting from the circuit generated by the conceptual metaphor. Then, expressions such as *Ho due anni più/meno di te* ('I am two years older/younger than you') were introduced by her within this conceptual framework, thus expanding upon the purely structural components of the unit. Typical exercises that showed the relation between surface language form and underlying conceptual structure were also written with great facility:

290.   *Quanti anni hanno i tuoi amici e come li portano?*
('How old are your friends, and how do they look for their age?')

291. *Chi ha più/meno anni di te?*
     (Who is older/younger than you?')

292. *Quanti ne hanno?*
     ('How old are they?')

Fill-ins, completions, multiple choices, etc. were also designed to bring out the conceptual structure of the dialogue. This mechanical practice component was followed by typical role-playing and textual analysis activities. Without going here into details, suffice it to say that the Middlebury experiment showed that the notion of semiotic competence is as teachable and usable in the creation of units as is any other pedagogical notion. By simply structuring designated units of study around conceptual networks and then by presenting the appropriate grammar and communication patterns of the language as reflexes of these, the result seems to be a pedagogical product that is as usable as is any other kind of pedagogical artifact.

Suggestions exist in the relevant pedagogical literature that fit in nicely with the idea of conceptual fluency. Masella and Portner (1981), for instance, explore ways in which Italian terms referring to the human body can be extended to cover large stretches of the conceptual territory charted by these terms. Maiguashca (1988) demonstrates how contrasting native-language metaphorical vehicles with the target language will prove to be effective in imparting conceptual fluency. Shibles (1989) shows how easily metaphorical vehicles for emotion in German can be compared to English ones for pedagogical purposes in ways that are very similar to the ones suggested here. And Nuessel and Cicogna (1993) illustrate how metaphorical networks can be used as the basis of teaching new material.

As a concrete example of how to relate surface grammar to underlying conceptual structure consider the following sentences:

293. I have been living here *since* 1980.
294. I have known Lucy *since* November.
295. I have not been able to sleep *since* Monday.
296. I have been living here *for* 22 years.
297. I have known Lucy *for* nine months.

298.   I have not been able to sleep *for* five days.

An analysis of the complements that follow *since* and *for* reveals that those that follow the former are "points in time", i.e. they are complements that reflect a metaphorical conception of time as a "point" on a "timeline" which shows specific years, months, etc.: *1980, November, Monday*, etc. Complements that follow *for*, on the other hand, reflect a conception of time as a "quantity": *fifteen years, nine months, five days*, etc. These two metaphorical concepts—[time is a point on a line] and [time is a quantity]—can now be seen to have a specific effect at the level of syntax by motivating a grammatical dichotomy—complements introduced by *since* are reflexes of [time is a point on a line]; those introduced by *for* are reflexes of [time is a quantity]. This is, in fact, the kind of rule of grammar that allows the teacher to relate how two specific domains of conceptualization have worked their way into the grammatical surface structure. In a word, this rule stipulates how a grammatical dichotomy reflexivizes a conceptual dichotomy.

In Italian, on the other hand, this rule does not exist; *da* is used in both instances. In all cases, (293)-(298), only *da* is used: *Vivo qui dal 1980*; *Vivo qui da quindici anni*, and so on. Students of Italian will be in a better position to avoid making typical errors such as **Vivo qui per quindici anni*, when they learn to conceptualize *time* in Italian appropriately, grasping the conceptual differences between "time in English" and "time in Italian". Explaining the phenomenon of *da* in such cases in any other way (e.g. in purely grammatical or lexical terms) continues to be a source of frustration. This was borne out, albeit only tentatively, by a classroom study conducted at the Ontario Institute for Studies in Education in 1998. Fourteen student-teachers of Italian were divided into two equal groups: group **A** was instructed to teach this area of grammar according to traditional text-book explanations (which focused on the verbal tense in itself); group **B** was instructed to teach it conceptually in the manner just described. The teaching took place during a practice-teaching session. At the end of the session, which lasted 3 weeks, the students in each classroom were given a simple written cloze test, consisting of a paragraph in which 15 prepositions were missing. Of the 15 slots 6 had to be filled-in with *da* in reference to the two concepts of *time* discussed above. The other slots were there as distracters. Group **A** had a total of 79 students, group **B** had 69. In group **A** only 26 of the 79 students, or 32.9% filled in the 6 slots with the correct preposition; in group **B**, on the other hand, 62 of the 69 students, or 89.9% filled in the 6 slots correctly. The same experiment was repeated the year after with a different group of 9 teachers and different classrooms with similar results: the students taught with the traditional view of this point of grammar scored 38.5%, those taught with a conceptual focus scored 92.3%.

As one other example, consider the selection of certain verbs in particular types of sentences in Italian. The verb *fare* 'to make' is used to convey a weather situation—*fa caldo* (literally) 'it makes hot', *fa freddo* (literally) 'it makes cold'. The physical state of 'hotness' and 'coldness' is conveyed instead by the verb *essere* 'to be' when referring to objects—*è caldo* 'it is hot', *è freddo* 'it is cold'—and by *avere* 'to have' when referring to people—*ha caldo* 'he/she is hot', *ha freddo* 'he/she is cold'. The use of one verb or the other—*fare, essere,* or *avere*—is motivated by an underlying metaphorical conceptualization of bodies and the environment as [containers] and the conditions of 'hotness' and 'coldness' as [entities]. The [container] and [entity] schemas are the sources of the differential verbal selections. If the [container] is the environment, then the [entities] of 'hotness' and 'coldness' are *made* by Nature *(fa caldo, fa freddo)*; if it is a human being, then the body *has* them *(ha caldo, ha freddo)*; and if it is an object, then the object *is* their container *(è caldo, è freddo)*.

For the sake of historical accuracy, it should be mentioned that the idea of making concepts the basis of the teaching syllabus was implicit in the so-called notional-functional movement of the early 1970s (e.g. Van Ek 1975; Wilkins 1976). The methodologists within this movement deployed speech-act and notional typologies as the organizing frameworks for developing the syllabus. Throughout that decade, and for most of the 1980s, that new functionalism in language teaching was greeted with widespread enthusiasm throughout Europe and America. Unlike the traditional grammar-based methods, it provided the teacher with greater room for imparting conceptual fluency. But now that the wave of enthusiasm has passed, it has become obvious that notional-functional teaching left many gaps to fill and many important questions unanswered. In my view, the main problem with the "notions" delineated by the theorists was that they were not conceived in terms of semiotic competence. The teacher was simply given a typology of the notions with verbal illustrations. This in no way is intended to berate the excellent work done by those theorists. The research on metaphor that has now become so widely known was not as readily available at the time as it is today.

In applied semiotics, clearly, CA will come to have an increasingly larger role to play in the future for studying conceptual systems aiming to answer questions such as the following:

- To what extent do the conceptual systems of the native and target cultures overlap and contrast?

- What kinds of interferences are produced by the student's native conceptual system (interconceptual interference)?

- How much conceptual interference is generated by the target language itself (intraconceptual interference)?

- What are the surface structure features that reflexivize conceptual domains?

As discussed throughout this book, the notion of semiotic competence is not preclusive of mainstream approaches to SLA and SLT. However, it implies that stage-based syllabi are virtually useless in solving the *SLT dilemma*. Given the interconnectedness among denotative, connotative and metaphorical conceptual structures, it is impossible to separate the learning process into predetermined stages. Nevertheless, many of the techniques and materials found in traditional structural and communicative syllabi can be used, whenever appropriate. In a semiotic approach to SLT, both the learner and the teacher will have to use their common sense in deciding *what* and *how much* to learn at various points in a course. In high school and university courses, the *what* is often established in advance. This does not, however, preclude the use of the semiotic approach described in this book. In such courses, the teacher and learner can use the curriculum provided as a basis for exploring the relation between surface language grammar and cultural conceptualization. Although this is not an ideal situation to be in—as learners and teachers constantly find out—it is something that should not discourage teachers from, at the very least, treating aspects of the given curriculum in ways that have been discussed in this book. Pedagogical units could be developed exploiting the learners' inherent semiotic curiosity. This can be done with techniques such as the following:

- Grammatical structures could be shown as re-flexivizing concepts.

- Translation could be oriented towards clarifying the meanings of concepts through contrastive analysis.

- Pattern practice could be adjusted to reinforce the ways in which a concept is encoded in the surface grammar.

- Role-playing could be adapted to encourage the creative use of network analyses of discourse events.

- Dialogues could be written to exemplify how networks are translated into words and syntactic structures.

- Authentic texts, audio-visual aids, and computer software could be selected to exemplify the conceptual structures under consideration at a specific point in the course.

- Testing could be based on the evaluation of the learn-ers' ability to understand and use concepts appropriately.

5.4 Concluding remarks

As Henry Schogt (1988: 38) perceptively remarks, all languages "have meaningful units that articulate human experience into discrete elements". The study of the interconnection between such elements and human experience is the goal of semiotics. The importance of incorporating this semiotic attitude into mainstream SLA and SLT cannot be overemphasized. Attempts to solve the *SLT dilemma* in other ways have produced few truly effective outcomes.

This book has attempted to shed some light on how semiotics can be incorporated into SLT directly. It has been motivated by a desire to solve the *SLT dilemma* for over more than 25 years. Much work remains to be done on expanding the notions of semiotic competence and conceptual fluency. But it must be emphasized once again that this approach to SLT is not the "magic key" that will guarantee successful language learning. There are simply too many factors involved in the learning experience that enter into the picture. Like the good piano teacher, experienced language teachers know all too well that each student is different, that each learning task presents its own kinds of problems, and, thus, that *patience* is the operative word in all situations and contexts of learning.

With or without semiotics, modern instructional techniques have been rather successful in training language learners to gain a firm control over grammar and communication. So, the issue of whether grammatical syllabi and formalistic instructional styles are more or less productive than communicative or functional ones is, in my view, a moot one. As Savignon (1992) has suggested, it is perhaps more appropriate, and certainly more useful, to think of the two kinds of approaches as cooperative and complementary contributors to SLA in the classroom, not as antagonistic or mutually exclusive competitors.

The basic goal of semiotics in language education is to put the teacher and the learner in a position to see that different languages encode reality in ways that are at times identical, at others similar or complementary, and at others still, quite different. My final thought is, however, a caveat. No matter how scientific or theoretically sound a particular account of language might appear to be, it is always susceptible to the vagaries of its human congener. The present account is no different. It is based on my own research and pedagogical experiences.

The twentieth century produced some rather interesting hypotheses, constructs, and suggestions for modeling educational practices and curricula. The idea of incorporating semiotics into these practices and curricula is not new (see for instance Kress 1995). But the application of semiotic theory to the domain of SL education has rarely been contemplated. The attractive aspect of semiotic inquiry is that is geared towards investigating the premise that all knowledge is interconnected with representation. Signs are employed by human beings across cultures to represent and classify the world. The result is that knowledge structures the world over, no matter how seemingly diverse they might appear, are assembled with the same basic signifying properties.

Among the first to suggest a study of education as a semiotic process was Vygotsky, with whose words I started this book. As Davydov and Radzikhovskii (1985: 59) have observed, it is unfortunate that Vygotsky's suggestion has never really been developed; the two scholars express the wish that this "can be considered a weakness that can be overcome in the future". Their sentiment encapsulates verbatim what my own wish is for the future in the domain of language education.

Glossary of technical terms

A

abstract concept	a mental form whose external referent cannot be demonstrated or observed directly
acquisition	unconscious learning of a language
addressee	the intended receiver of a message
addresser	the originator of a message
alliteration	the repetition of the initial consonant sounds or features of words
alphabet	graphic code providing individual characters that stand for individual sounds (or sound combinations)
analogy	equivalence property of forms, by which one type of form can be replaced by another that is perceived as being comparable to it
anaphora	process of replacing previously-occurring words in a discourse with other words or particles so that repetition can be avoided
antonymy	process whereby meanings can be seen to convey something contrary or opposite
applied semiotics	the study of language learning from a semiotic perspective in view of converting semiotic theories into pedagogical practices
Army specialized training program	behaviorist language teaching method based on imitation and pattern practice, used to train army personnel during the Second World War
association	process of connecting concepts with one another
association-by-inference	associating concepts by a process of extension or perceived resemblance
association-by-sense	associating concepts on the basis of perceived common features

associationism	school of psychology claiming that learning and concept-formation is associative in nature
audiolingual method	second language teaching method based on behaviorist principles such as imitation, habit formation, and reinforcement
audiovisual method	second language teaching method that utilized film strips to present new material

B

basic concept	concept that has a typological function
behaviorism	school of psychology stressing the experimental study of observable behavior
binary opposition	minimal difference between two forms

C

cataphora	process of using words or particles in a discourse in anticipation of other words or particles so that repetition can be avoided
cerebral dominance	view that the left hemisphere of the brain is the dominant one for all the higher mental functions
character	alphabetic symbol
circuit	a group of concepts that are associated either by sense or inference
code	system of signifying elements which can be deployed to represent types of phenomena in specific ways
cognitive style	the particular way in which information and knowledge are processed
cognitive-code method	second language teaching method based on generativist principles such as rule-learning and linguistic competence
cognitivism	school of psychology stressing the study of mental processes independently of the physical behaviors they produce

communication	capacity to participate with other organisms in the reception and processing of specific kinds of signs
communicative competence	the ability to use language in specific situations
communicative syllabus	second language teaching syllabus based on speech functions
community counseling	humanistic second language teaching method in which the student is viewed as comparable to a client in therapy
conative	the effect that a message has on its receiver
concept	any meaning derived from a sign
conceptual fluency	the ability to put together messages in a conceptually-appropriate fashion
conceptual metaphor	generalized metaphorical formula that defines a specific abstraction
conceptual metonym	generalized metonymic formula that defines a specific abstraction
conceptual reorganization	process of reorganizing the forms of the native language in terms of the corresponding forms of the second language
concrete concept	mental concept whose external referent is demonstrable and observable in a direct way
connotation	extension of a sign over a new meaning domain that is recognized as entailing the features of the sign's meaning by implication
connotative chaining	discourse phenomenon whereby one concept suggests another related to it by association which, in turn, suggests another, and so on
contact	the physical mode in which a message is delivered
context	situation—physical, psychological, and social—in which a sign or text is used or occurs, or to which it refers
contrastive analysis	pedagogical technique consisting in identifying areas of contrast between the native and second languages
crisscrossing	feature of conceptual networks whereby concepts can be seen to crisscross

critical period hypothesis	hypothesis that language learning is completed by around the age of puberty
cultural modeling	the association of various source domains with one target domain, producing an overall, or culture-specific model, of the target domain
culture	the system of daily living that is held together by a signifying order (signs, codes, texts, figural assemblages forms)

D

decoding	use of a code to decipher meanings
deduction	process of applying a sign to a specific referent
denotation	initial, or intentional, meaning captured by a sign
differentiation	complete contrast between a native and second language form
direct method	second language teaching method stressing experiential learning and based on the idea that second language learning followed the same course as native language acquisition
distinctive feature	minimal element that makes up a form and which singularly or in combination with other distinctive features serves to differentiate its meaning from other forms

E

emotive	emotional intent of the addresser in the delivery of a message
encoding	use of a code to make forms, representations, and messages
error analysis	study of errors in the speech of second language learners

F

firstness	earliest strategy for knowing an object with the senses
focal color	a color category that is universal or associated with a universal sequencing of colors
form	a mental image, or an external representation of something

G

gambit.	conversational device used in a specific way (to indicate consent, to initiate a conversation, etc.)
generativism	school of linguistic based on the idea that grammar is a rule-governed system constituting an innate faculty of the brain
gesticulant	gesture accompanying speech
gesture	use of the hands, the arms, and to a lesser extent, the head, to make bodily forms of all kinds
grafting	associating concepts in different domains
grammar-translation	language teaching method in which grammar is taught by rules and practice is structured to unfold through translation exercises
ground	the meaning of a metaphor

H

holophrase	the one-word utterance produced by infants
homograph	word that is spelled exactly like another word
homophone	word that is pronounced exactly like another word
hypoicon	icon that is shaped by cultural convention but whose referent can nonetheless be figured out by those who are not members of the culture

I

icon	sign that simulates its referent in some way
iconicity	the process of representing referents with iconic signs
image schema	mental impression of locations, movements, shapes, etc.
index	sign that establishes a contiguity with its referent (pointing it out, showing its relation to other things, etc.)
indexicality	process of representing referents with indexical signs
induction	process of deriving a concept from particular facts of instances
inflection	variations or changes that words undergo to indicate their relations with other words
intercodality	interconnection of one code to other codes
interconnectedness principle	principle claiming that concepts are interconnected to each other in various ways
interlanguage	type of speech manifested typically by second language learners
intertextuality	referents present in one text that allude to referents in other texts
irony	use of words to convey a message that contradicts their meaning
isomorphism	virtual synonymy between any forms and concepts of the native and second languages

L

language acquisition device	notion that language acquisition is governed by a mental faculty designed specifically for the purpose
langue	knowledge of the language code
learning	process of consciously learning a language
linguistic competence	knowledge of language as a system

looping	feature of certain networks in which certain concepts can be seen to go into a loop

M

meaning	particular concept elicited by a specific sign
mental image	mental outline of something (a shape, a sound, etc.)
message	the purpose or objective of a discourse event
metalingual	use of language to refer to itself
metaphor	using a concrete concept to describe an abstract one
metaphorical circuit	conceptual circuit in discourse generated by metaphorical thinking
method notion	notion in second language education that teaching practices can be designed to reflect systematically a specific view of learning
metonymy	use of an entity to refer to another that is related to it
mode	manner in which a form is encoded (visual, auditory, etc.)
modeling systems theory	theory which posits the presence of species-specific modeling systems that allow a species to produce the forms it needs for understanding the world in its own way
morpheme	minimal meaningful form in a language
myth	any story or narrative that aims to explain the origin of something
mythic circuit	conceptual circuit generated by a mythic theme, plot, character, etc.

N

name	form that identifies a human being or, by connotative extension, an animal, an object (such as a commercial product), and event (such as a hurricane)

narrative	something told or written, such as an account, story, tale, etc.
narrative circuit	conceptual circuit generated by a theme, plot, character, etc. derived from a narrative
native language	first language acquired
natural approach	second language teaching approach stressing the need to separate acquisitional from conscious learning processes in pedagogy
natural method	second language teaching approach based on the view that second language learning should follow the same course as native language acquisition
natural order	view that there is a sequence of stages through which second language acquisition must pass
navigation	notion that discourse competence is tied to the ability to access the underlying conceptual networks that sustain it
negative transfer	transfer of a feature of the native language to the second language that is in contrast with it
network	system of interconnections related to a specific concept
network domain	system of interconnections among concepts
network theory	technique for showing how concepts tend to become associated with each other
node	concept in a network circuit

O

onomatopoeia	vocal iconicity
ontological image schema	image schema underlying the derivation of metaphors perceived to have either the structural properties of entities, substances, containers, impediments, etc. or the characteristics of physical processes and forms—plants, movements, etc.
opposition	process by which forms are differentiated through a minimal change in their signifiers

oral method	second language teaching method stressing oral conversation
orientational image schema	image schema underlying the derivation of metaphors perceived to have orientational structure—up, down, back, front, near, far, etc.
overlapping	partial congruence between a native and a second language concept or form

P

paradigmaticity	a differentiation property of forms
parole	the use of language in speech situations
path analysis	analysis of the circuitry underlying a specific discourse event
phatic	use of speech to make contact, to initiate a conversation, etc.
phoneme	minimal unit of sound in a language that serves to distinguish meaning
pictograph	pictorial representation of a referent
pictographic writing	writing in pictures
poetic	speech that is highly figurative and iconic
primary modeling system	instinctive ability to model the sensible properties of things (i.e. properties that can be sensed)
proficiency movement	second language teaching movement stressing an integration of linguistic and communicative syllabi

R

reading method	deductive second language teaching method stressing grammar, translation, and reading
referent	an object, event, feeling, idea, etc. that is represented by a sign
referential	use of language to refer to something other than itself

referential domain	a class of objects, events, feelings, ideas, etc. represented by a form
reflexivization.	process of converting conceptual structure into surface grammar and vocabulary
reform movement	educational movement stressing the use of inductive learning
representation	process of ascribing a form to some referent

S

scenario approach	second language teaching method in which students decide how to role-play some scenario
second language	any language learned after the firs or native language
second language acquisition	process of acquiring the second language mainly through unconscious processes
second language learning	process of consciously learning a second language
second language teaching	practice of teaching second languages systematically
secondness	ability to refer to the objects through indication or verbal reference
semiosis	capacity of a species to produce and comprehend the specific types of models it requires for processing and codifying perceptual input in its own way
semiotic competence	ability to access the codes of the signifying order in order to create conceptual circuitry for the delivery of message
semiotics	the science of signs
sign	something that stands for something else
signification	relation that holds between a sign and its referent
signified	part of a sign that is referred to (the referent)
signifier	part of a sign that does the referring (the form)

signifying order	interconnected system of signs, texts, codes, and figural forms
silent way	second language teaching method stressing the need for teachers to be more silent
source domain	set of vehicles (concrete forms) that is used to deliver the meaning of an abstract metaphorical concept
speech	expressed language
speech act	use of speech to accomplish some objective
structural image schema	image schema that combines ontological and orientational properties
structural syllabus	language teaching syllabus in which grammatical structures and vocabulary are arranged in order of increasing complexity
structuralism	the approach in semiotics that views signs as reflexes of intellectual and emotional structures in the human psyche
structure	any repeatable or predictable aspect of signs
subordinate concept	concept needed for specialized purposes
substitution	process of replacing one form for another at the surface-structure level of language
suggestopedia	second language teaching method stressing the role of subliminal processes in learning
superordinate concept	concept with a highly general referential function
surface code	grammar or lexicon of a language
surface structure	the level at which concepts surface as words, tones, phrases, etc.
syllabus	compendium of items to be learned in a language course
symbol	sign that stands arbitrarily or conventionally for its referent
symbolicity	the process of representing referents with symbolic forms
synonym	form that is perceived to have the same meaning as some other form
syntagmaticity	combinatory property of forms

syntax	syntagmatic structure in language

T

tag question	form added to the end of a sentence that is designed to seek consent, agreement, etc.
target domain	what a metaphor is about (abstract concept that is metaphorized)
telegraphic stage	stage of language acquisition characterized by the making of brief phrases resembling telegraphic messages
text	something put together to represent complex (non-unitary) referents
thirdness	abstract form of knowing
topic	the subject of a metaphor
total physical response	second language teaching method that stresses the use of language to accomplish physical actions
transfer theory	view that second language acquisition unfolds as a process characterized by the transfer of native language habits, forms, categories, etc. to the second language

U

universal grammar	theory that language consists of a set of universal inbuilt grammatical principles present in the brain at birth

V

vehicle	the part of the metaphor that is associated with the subject
verbal fluency	ability to control the grammar and communicative formulas of the second language

Works cited and general bibliography

Agard, Frederick and Di Pietro, Robert J.

   1965a   *The Sounds of English and Italian.* Chicago: University of Chicago Press.

   1965b   *The Grammatical Structures of English and Italian.* Chicago: University of Chicago Press.

Allen, J. B. P.

   1983.   A three-level curriculum model for second language education. *Canadian Modern Language Review* 4: 23-43.

   1988.   The development of instructional models in second language education. *Annual Review of Applied Linguistics* 9: 179-192.

Allport, G. W.

   1965   *Pattern and Growth in Personality.* New York: Holt

Allwood, Jens and Peter Gärdenfors (eds.)

   1998   *Cognitive Semantics: Meaning and Cognition.* Amsterdam: John Benjamins.

Anthony, E. M.

   1963   Approach, method and technique. *English Language Teaching* 17: 63-67.

Anttila, Raimo

   1977   *Analogy.* The Hague: Mouton.

Appelbaum, David

   1990   *Voice.* Albany: State University of New York Press.

Argyle, Michael

   1988   *Bodily Communication.* New York: Methuen.

Arndt, H. and H. W. Pesch

   1984   Nonverbal communication and visual teaching aids: A perceptual approach. *Modern Language Journal*, 68 1984: 28-36.

Arnheim, Rudolf

   1969   *Visual Thinking.* Berkeley: University of California Press.

Arries, Jonathan F.

   1994   Constructing culture study units: A blueprint and practical tools. *Foreign Language Annals* 27: 523-34.

Asch, Solomon

1955   On the uses of metaphor in the description of persons. In: H. Werner (ed.), *On Expressive Language*, 29-39. Worcester: Clark University Press.

1958   The metaphor: A psychological inquiry. In: R. Tagiuri and L. Petrullo (eds.), *Person Perception and Interpersonal Behavior*, 28-42. Stanford: Stanford University Press.

Asher, James J.

1965   The strategy of the total physical response: An application to learning Russian. *International Review of Applied Linguistics* 3: 292-9.

1969   The optimal age to learn a foreign language. *Modern Language Journal* 53: 334-341.

1972   Children's first language as a model for second language learning. *Modern Language Journal* 56:133-9.

1977   *Learning Another Language Through Actions: The Complete Teacher's Guidebook*. Los Gatos: Sky Oaks.

1988   *Brainswitching: A Skill for the 21st Century*. Los Gatos, Ca.: Sky Oaks Productions.

Asher, James J., Joe Anne Kuudo, and Rita De la Torre

1974   Learning a second language through commands: The second field test. *Modern Language Journal* 58: 24-32.

Austin, J. L.

1962. *How to Do Things with Words*. Cambridge, Mass.: Harvard University Press.

Ausubel, D. A.

1965   Adult vs. children in second language learning: Psychological considerations. *Modern Language Journal* 48: 420-24.

1967   *Educational psychology: A Cognitive View*. New York: Holt, Rinehart and Winston.

Bailey, K. M.

1985   Classroom-centered teaching and learning. In: M. Celce-Murcia (ed.), *Beyond Basics*, 109-123. Rowley, Mass.: Newbury House.

Balboni, Paolo

1985   *Guida all'esame delle lingue straniere*. Brescia: La Scuola.

1988   *Gli insegnamenti linguistici nella scuola italiana*. Padova: Liviana Editrice.

1991   *Tecniche didattiche e processi di apprendimento linguistico*. Padova: Liviana Editrice.

1994   *Didattica dell'italiano a stranieri*. Roma: Bonacci.

Bancroft, Jane

1972   Foreign language teaching in Bulgaria. *Canadian Modern Language Review* 28: 9-13.

1978   The Lozanov method and its American applications. *Modern Language Journal* 62: 167-75.

1995   *The Two-Sided Mind: Teaching and Suggestopedia*. Washington: Eric Clearing House.

Barasch, Ronald M. and James C. Vaughan (eds.)

1994   *Beyond the Monitor Model. Comments on Current Theory and Practice in Second language Acquisition*. Boston: Heinle and Heinle.

Barthes, Roland

1957   *Mythologies*. Paris: Seuil.

1964   *Éléments de sémiologie*. Paris: Seuil.

1967   *Système de la mode*. Paris: Seuil.

1977   *Image-Music-Text*. London: Fontana.

Benedict, H.

1979   Early lexical development: comprehension and production. *Journal of Child Language* 6: 183-200.

Berko, Jean

1958   The child's learning of English morphology. *Word* 14: 150-177.

Berlin, Brent and Paul Kay

1969   *Basic Color Terms*. Berkeley: University of California Press.

Bialystock, Ellen (ed.)

1991   *Language Processing in Bilingual Children*. Cambridge: Cambridge University Press.

Bialystock, Ellen and Ken Hakuta

1994   *In Other Words: The Science and Psychology of Second-Language Acquisition*. New York: Basic.

Birdwhistell, R.

1970   *Kinesics and Context: Essays on Body Motion Communication*. Harmondsworth: Penguin.

Black, Max

1962   *Models and Metaphors*. Ithaca: Cornell University Press.

Blair, Robert W. (ed.)

  1982   *Innovative Approaches to Language Teaching.* Rowley Mass.: New-
          bury House Publishers.

Bloomfield, Leonard

  1933   *Language.* New York: Holt.

  1942   *Outline Guide for the Practical Study of Foreign Languages.* Balti-
          more: Linguistic Society of America.

Bloor, T.

  1986   What do language students know about grammar? *British Journal of
          Language Teaching* 24: 157-160.

Bogen, J. E.

  1975   Some educational aspects of hemispheric specialization. *UCLA Edu-
          cator* 12: 24-32.

Boysson-Bardies, B. de and M. M. Vihman

  1991   Adaptation to language: Evidence from babbling and first words in
          four languages. *Language* 67: 297-319.

Braine, M.

  1963   The ontogeny of English phrase structure: The first phase. *Language*
          39: 1-13.

  1971   The acquisition of language in infant and child. In: C. E. Reed (ed.),
          The Learning of Language, 34-56. New York: Appleton-Century-
          Crofts.

Bremer, J. and H. Roodenburg, H. (ed.)

  1991   *A Cultural History of Gesture.* Ithaca: Cornell University Press.

Bressan, Dino

  1987   Enigmatic devices in English-Italian translation. *Multilingua* 6: 69-
          75.

Brière, E. J.

  1968   *A Psycholinguistic Study of Phonological Interference.* The Hague:
          Mouton.

Britton, J.

  1970   *Language and Learning.* Harmondsworth: Penguin.

Broca, Pierre Paul

  1861   Remarques sur le siège de la faculté du langage articulé suivies d'une
          observation d'aphémie. *Bulletin de la Société d'Anatomie* 36: 320-
          357.

184   *Works cited and general bibliography*

Broselow, E.

    1988   Second language acquisition. In: F. J. Newmeyer (ed.), *Language: Psychological and Biological Aspects*, 194-209. Cambridge: Cambridge University Press.

Brown, H. Douglas

    1994   *Principles of Language Learning and Teaching*. Englewood Cliffs, N. J.: Prentice-Hall.

Brown, H. Douglas and Susan Gonzo (eds.)

    1995   *Readings on Second Language Acquisition*. Englewood Cliffs, NJ: Prentice Hall Regents.

Brown, Roger

    1958a   *Words and Things: An Introduction to Language*. New York: The Free Press.

    1958b   How shall a thing be called? *Psychological Review* 65: 14-21.

    1970   *Psycholinguistics*. New York: Free Press.

    1973.   *A First Language*. Cambridge, Mass.: Harvard University Press.

    1976   Reference: In memorial tribute to Eric Lenneberg. *Cognition* 4: 125-153.

    1986   *Social Psychology*. New York: Free Press.

Bruner, Jerome

    1983   *Child Talk*. New York: W. W. Norton.

    1986   *Actual Minds, Possible Worlds*. Cambridge, Mass.: Harvard University Press.

    1990   *Acts of Meaning*. Cambridge, Mass.: Harvard University Press.

Bühler, Karl

    1934   *Sprachtheorie: Die Darstellungsfunktion der Sprache*. Jena: Fischer.

Burt, Marina K and Carol Kiparsky

    1972   *The Gooficon: A Repair Manual for English*. Rowley, Mass.: Newbury House.

Byram, M.

    1989   *Cultural Studies in Foreign Language Education*. Philadelphia: Multilingual Matters, Ltd.

Cameron, Lynne and Graham Low

    1999   *Researching and Applying Metaphor*. Cambridge: Cambridge University Press.

Canale, Michael

1984   On Some theoretical frameworks for language proficiency. In: C. Rivera (ed.), *Language Proficiency and Academic Achievement*, 28-40. Clevedon: Multilingual Matters.

Canale, Michael and Merrill Swain

1979   *Communicative Approaches to Second Language Teaching and Testing*. Toronto: Ministry of Education.

Carroll, John B.

1971   Current issues in psycholinguistics and second language teaching. *TESOL Quarterly* 5: 273-280.

1981   Conscious and automatic process in language learning. *Canadian Modern Language Review* 37: 462-74.

Celce-Murcia, M.

1991   Grammar pedagogy in second and foreign language teaching. *TESOL Quarterly* 25: 459-480.

Chastain, Kenneth

1971   *The Development of Modern Language Skills: Theory to Practice*. Philadelphia: Center for Curriculum Development.

1975   Affective and ability factors in second language acquisition. *Language Learning* 24: 153-161.

Cherwitz, R. and J. Hikins

1986   *Communication and Knowledge: An Investigation in Rhetorical Epistemology*. Columbia: University of South Carolina Press.

Chomsky, Noam

1957   *Syntactic Structures*. The Hague: Mouton.

1965   *Aspects of the Theory of Syntax*. Cambridge, Mass.: MIT Press.

1982   *Some Concepts and Consequences of the Theory of Government and Binding*. Cambridge, Mass.: MIT Press.

1986   *Knowledge of Language: Its Nature, Origin, and Use*. New York: Praeger.

Cicogna, Caterina, Marcel Danesi, and Anthony Mollica (eds.)

1992   *Problem Solving in Second-Language Teaching*. Welland: Soleil.

Clahsen, H.

1990   The comparative study of first and second language development. *Studies in Second Language Acquisition* 12: 135-153.

Clement, R., R. C. Gardner, and P. C. Smythe

1980   Social and individual factors in second language acquisition. *Canadian Journal of Behavioural Science* 12: 292-302.

Comrie, B.

> 1990   Second language acquisition and language universals research. *Studies in Second Language Acquisition* 12: 209-218.

Connor, Ulla

> 1996   *Contrastive Rhetoric: Cross-Cultural Aspects of Second-Language Writing*. Cambridge: Cambridge University Press.

Cook, Vivian

> 1991   *Second Language Learning and Language Teaching*. London, New York, Melbourne and Auckland: Edward Arnold.

Corder, S. Pit

> 1971   Idiosyncratic dialects and error analysis. *International Review of Applied Linguistics* 9: 147-159.

> 1981   *Error Analysis and Inter-Language*. Oxford: Oxford University Press.

Craig, C. (ed.)

> 1986   *Noun Classes and Categorization*. Amsterdam: John Benjamins.

Cruttenden, A.

> 1974   An experiment involving comprehension of intonation in children from 7 to 10. *Journal of Child Language* 1: 221-231.

Cummins, James

> 1979   Linguistic interdependence and the educational development of bilingual children. *Review of Educational Research* 49: 222-251.

> 1984   *Bilingualism and Special Education: Issues in Assessment and Pedagogy*. Clevedon: Multilingual Matters.

> 1986   Empowering minority students: A framework for intervention. *Harvard Educational Review* 56: 18-36.

Cummins, James and Marcel Danesi

> 1990   *Heritage Languages: The Development and Denial of Canada's Linguistic Resources*. Toronto: Garamond Press.

Cummins, James and Merrill Swain

> 1986   *Bilingualism in Education*. London: Longman.

Curran, Charles A.

> 1976   *Counseling-Learning in Second Languages*. Apple River, Ill.: Apple River Press.

Danesi Marcel

1992   Metaphor and classroom second language learning. *Romance Languages Annual* 3: 189-193.

1993a   Whither contrastive analysis? *Canadian Modern Language Review* 50: 37-46.

1993b   Metaphorical competence in second language acquisition and second language teaching: The neglected dimension. In: J. E. Alatis (ed.), *Language Communication and Social Meaning*, 234-254. Washington, D.C.: Georgetown University Press.

1994   Recent research on metaphor and the teaching of Italian. *Italica* 71: 453 - 464.

1995   Learning and teaching languages: The role of conceptual fluency. *International Journal of Applied Linguistics* 5: 1-12.

1999   The dimensionality of metaphor. *Sign Systems Studies* 27: 60-87.

Danesi, Marcel and Christopher De Sousa

1995   Why has the debate on bilingual education been rekindled? In: K. A. McLeod (ed.), *Multicultural Education: The State of the Art*, 1-10. Winnipeg: Canadian Association of Second Language Teachers.

Danesi, Marcel and Robert J. Di Pietro

1991   *Contrastive Analysis for the Contemporary Second Language Classroom*. Toronto: OISE Press.

Danesi, Marcel and Anthony Mollica

1998   Conceptual fluency theory and second language teaching. *Mosaic* 5/2: 1-12.

Danesi, Marcel and Paul Perron

1999   *Analyzing Cultures: An Introduction and Handbook*. Bloomington: Indiana University Press.

Danesi, Marcel and Donato Santeramo

1995   *Deictic Verbal Constructions*. Urbino: Centro Internazionale di Semiotica e di Linguistica.

Daniels, H. (ed.)

1996   *An Introduction to Vygotsky*. London: Routledge.

Davydov, V. V. and L. A. Radzikhovskii

1985   Vygotsky's theory and the activity oriented approach in psychology. In: J. V. Wertsch (ed.), *Culture, Communication and Cognition: Vygotskian Perspectives*, 59-69. Cambridge: Cambridge University Press.

De Villiers, J. G., and P. A. De Villiers

    1978   *Language Acquisition*. Cambridge, Mass.: Harvard University Press.

Deane, Paul

    1992   *Grammar in Mind and Brain: Explorations in Cognitive Syntax*. Berlin: Mouton de Gruyter.

Deely, John

    1990   *Basics of Semiotics*. Bloomington: Indiana University Press.

Dewey, John

    1916   *Democracy in Education*. New York: The Free Press.

Di Pietro, Robert J.

    1971   *Language Structures in Contrast*. Rowley, Mass.: Newbury House.

    1987   *Strategic Interaction*. Cambridge: Cambridge University Press.

Diadori, Pierangela

    1990   *Senza parole: 100 gesti degli italiani*. Roma: Bonacci.

Diller, Karl

    1978   *The Language Teaching Controversy*. Rowley Mass.: Newbury House Publishers.

Dirven, René and Marjolijn Verspoor

    1998   *Cognitive Exploration of Language and Linguistics*. Amsterdam: John Benjamins.

Dulay, Heidi, Marina K. Burt, and Stephen Krashen

    1982   *Language Two*. Oxford: Oxford University Press.

Dundes, Alan

    1972   Seeing is believing. *Natural History* 81: 9-12.

Dusková, L.

    1969   On sources of errors in foreign language learning. *International Review of Applied Linguistics* 7: 11-36.

Eco, Umberto

    1976   *A Theory of Semiotics*. Bloomington: Indiana University Press.

Ellis, Rod

    1997   *Second Language Acquisition*. Oxford: Oxford University Press.

Entwistle, W.

    1981   *Styles of Learning and Teaching*. New York: John Wiley.

Faerch, C., K. Haastrup, and R. Phillipson

    1984   *Learner Language and Language Learning*. Clevedon: Multilingual Matters.

Fauconnier, Gilles

1985   *Mental Spaces*. Cambridge: Cambridge University Press.

1997   *Mappings in Thought and Language*. Cambridge: Cambridge University Press.

Fauconnier, Gilles and Eve Sweetser (eds.)

1996   *Spaces, Worlds, and Grammar*. Chicago: University of Chicago Press.

Feez, Susan

1998   *Text-Based Syllabus Design*. New South Wales: Ames.

Felder, Richard M. and Eunice R. Henriques

1995   Learning and teaching styles in foreign and second language education. *Foreign Language Annals* 28: 21-31.

Firth, J. R.

1957   *Papers in Linguistics: 1934-1951*. Oxford: Oxford University Press.

Fisiak, J. (ed.)

1981   *Contrastive Analysis and the Language Teacher*. Oxford: Pergamon Press.

Flege, J. L.

1987   A Critical Period for Learning to pronounce Foreign Languages? *Applied Linguistics* 8: 162-177.

Foucault, Michel

1972   *The Archeology of Knowledge*, trans. by A. M. Sheridan Smith. New York: Pantheon.

Fries, Charles F.

1927   *The Teaching of the English Language*. New York: Appleton Century.

1945   *Teaching and Learning English as a Foreign Language*. Ann Arbor: University of Michigan Press.

Garza-Cuarón, Beatriz

1991   *Connotation and Meaning*. Berlin: Mouton de Gruyter.

Gass, Susan

1983   The development of L2 intuitions. *TESOL Quarterly* 17: 273-291.

Gass, Susan and C. Madden (eds.)

1985   *Input in Second Language Acquisition*. Rowley, Mass.: Newbury House.

Gass, Susan and Larry Selinker

> 1994   *Second Language Acquisition: An Introductory Course.* Hillsdale: Lawrence Erlbaum Associates.

Gattegno, Caleb

> 1972   *Teaching Foreign Languages in Schools: The Silent Way.* New York: Education Solutions.

> 1976   *The Common Sense of Teaching Foreign Languages.* New York: Educational Solutions.

Genesee, Fred

> 1987   *Learning through Two Languages.* Rowley, Mass.: Newbury House.

George, H. V.

> 1972   *Common Errors in Language Learning.* Rowley, Mass.: Newbury House.

Germain, Claude

> 1993   *Évolution de l'enseignement des langues: 5000 ans d'histoire.* La Salle: Hurtubise.

Gibbs, Raymond W.

> 1994   *The Poetics of Mind: Figurative Thought, Language and Understanding.* Cambridge: Cambridge University Press.

Goatley, Andrew

> 1997   *The Language of Metaphors.* London: Routledge.

Grabe, W.

> 1991   Current developments in second language reading research. *TESOL Quarterly* 25: 375-406.

Gregg, Kevin

> 1984   Krashen's monitor and Occam's razor. *Applied Linguistics* 5: 79-100.

Greimas, Algirdas J.

> 1987   *On Meaning: Selected Essays in Semiotic Theory*, trans. by P. Perron and F. Collins. Minneapolis: University of Minnesota Press.

Haden Elgin, Suzette

> 2000   *The Language Imperative.* Cambridge, Mass.: Perseus.

Hall, Edward T.

> 1966   *The Hidden Dimension.* New York: Doubleday.

Halliday, M. A. K.

> 1973   *Explorations in the Functions of Language.* London: Edward Arnold.

1975   *Learning How to Mean: Explorations in the Development of Language.* London: Edward Arnold.

1985   *Introduction to Functional Grammar.* London: Arnold.

Halliday, M. A. K., A. McIntosh, and P. Strevens

1964   *The Linguistic Sciences and Language Teaching.* London: Longman.

Hamers, J. F. and M. H. A. Blanc

1989   *Bilinguality and Bilingualism* Cambridge: Cambridge University Press.

Henry, A. R.

1993   *Second Language Rhetorics in Process: A Comparison of Arabic, Chinese, and Spanish.* New York: Peter Lang.

Hinkel, Eli

1999   *Culture in Second Language Teaching and Learning.* Cambridge: Cambridge University Press.

House, J.

1996   Developing pragmatic fluency in English as a foreign language: Routines and metapragmatic awareness. *Studies in Second Language Acquisition* 18: 225-252.

Hurford, J. R.

1991   The evolution of a critical period for language acquisition. *Cognition* 40: 159-201.

Hymes, Dell 1971. *On Communicative Competence.* Philadelphia: University of Pennsylvania Press.

Indurkhya, B.

1992   *Metaphor and Cognition.* Dordrecht: Kluwer.

Ingram, David

1989   *First Language Acquisition: Method, Description, and Explanation.* Cambridge: Cambridge University Press.

Inhelder, B. and J. Piaget

1958   *The Growth of Logical Thinking from Childhood through Adolescence.* New York: Basic.

Jackson, J. H.

1874   On the nature and duality of the brain. *Medical Press and Circular* 1: 19-41.

1878   On affectives of speech from disease of the brain. *Brain* 1: 304-330.

Jacobs, B.

1988   Neurobiological differentiation of primary and secondary language acquisition. *Studies in Second Language Acquisition* 10: 303-337.

1995   Dis-integrating perspectives of language acquisition: A response to Eubank and Gregg. *Studies in Second Language Acquisition* 17: 65-72.

Jakobovits, L. A.

1970   *Foreign Language Learning: A Psycholinguistic Analysis of the Issues.* Rowley, Mass.: Newbury House.

Jakobson, Roman

1942   *Kindersprache, Aphasie und algemeine Lautgesetze.* Uppsala: Almqvist and Wiksell.

1960   Linguistics and poetics. In: Thomas A. Sebeok (ed.), *Style and Language*, 34-45. Cambridge, Mass.: MIT Press.

James, Carl

1980   *Contrastive Analysis.* London: Longman.

Jeffries, S.

1985   English grammar terminology as an obstacle to second language learning. *Modern Language Journal* 69: 385-390.

Jesperson, Otto

1904   *How to Teach a Foreign Language.* London: Allen and Unwin.

Johnson, K.

1996.   *Language Teaching & Skill Learning.* Oxford: Blackwell.

Johnson, Mark

1987   *The Body in the Mind: The Bodily Basis of Meaning, Imagination, and Reason.* Chicago: University of Chicago Press.

Johnson, S.

1979   *Nonverbal Communication in the Teaching of Foreign Languages.* Dissertation, Indiana University.

Jones, Robert

1982   *Physics as Metaphor.* New York: New American Library.

Joos, Martin

1967   *The Five Clocks.* New York: Harcourt, Brace and World.

Kaplan, Robert D.

1966   Cultural thought Patterns in Inter-Cultural Education. *Language Learning* 16: 1 - 20.

1978   Contrastive rhetoric: Some hypothesis." *Review of Applied Linguistics* 39: 61 - 72.

Kelly, L. G.

1969   *25 Centuries of Language Teaching*. Rowley, Mass.: Newbury House.

Kövecses, Z.

1986   *Metaphors of Anger, Pride, and Love: A Lexical Approach to the Structure of Concepts.* Amsterdam: Benjamins.

1988   *The Language of Love: The Semantics of Passion in Conversational English.* London: Associated University Presses.

1990   *Emotion Concepts.* New York: Springer.

Krampen, Martin

1991   *Children's Drawings: Iconic Coding of the Environment.* New York: Plenum.

Kramsch, Claire

1998   *Language and Culture.* Oxford: Oxford University Press.

Krashen, Stephen D.

1973   Lateralization, language learning and the critical period: Some new evidence. *Language Learning* 23: 63-74.

1975   The development of cerebral dominance and language learning: More new evidence. In: D. Dato (ed.), *Developmental Psycholinguistics*, 179-192. Washington, D. C.: Georgetown University Press.

1982   *Principles and Practice in Second Language Acquisition.* Oxford: Pergamon.

1985   *The Input Hypothesis.* London : Longman.

1991   *Bilingual Education: A Focus on Current Research.* Washington, D.C.: National Clearinghouse for Bilingual Education.

Krashen, Stepehn D. and Tracy Terrell

1983   *The Natural Approach: Language Acquisition in the Classroom.* Oxford: Pergamon.

Kress, Gunther

1995   *Making Signs and Making Subjects: The English Curriculum and Social Futures.* London: Institute of Education.

Kroll, B. (ed.)

1990   *Second Language Writing: Research Insight for the Classroom.* Cambridge: Cambridge University Press.

Kufner, H. L.

1962   *The Grammatical Structures of English and German.* Chicago: University of Chicago Press.

Kuhn, Thomas S.

1970   *The Structure of Scientific Revolutions.* Chicago: University of Chicago Press.

Lado, Robert

1957   *Linguistics Across Cultures: Applied Linguistics for Language Teachers.* Ann Arbor: University of Michigan Press.

1964   *Language Teaching: A Scientific Approach.* Toronto: McGraw-Hill, Inc.

Lakoff, George

1987   *Women, Fire, and Dangerous Things: What Categories Reveal about the Mind.* Chicago: University of Chicago Press.

Lakoff, George and Mark Johnson

1980   *Metaphors We Live By.* Chicago: Chicago University Press.

1999   *Philosophy in the Flesh.* New York: Basic.

Lakoff, George and Mark Turner

1989   *More than Cool Reason: A Field Guide to Poetic Metaphor.* Chicago: University of Chicago Press.

Langacker, Ronald W.

1987   *Foundations of Cognitive Grammar.* Stanford: Stanford University Press.

1990   *Concept, Image, and Symbol: The Cognitive Basis of Grammar.* Berlin: Mouton de Gruyter.

Langer, Susanne K.

1948   *Philosophy in a New Key.* Cambridge: Harvard University Press.

Larsen-Freeman, Diane

1986   *Techniques and Principles in Language Teaching.* Oxford: Oxford U. P.

Leech, Geoffrey

1981   *Semantics: The Study of Meaning.* Harmondsworth: Penguin.

Leki, I.

1991   Twenty-five years of contrastive rhetoric: Text analysis and writing pedagogies. *TESOL Quarterly* 25: 123-143.

Lenneberg, Eric

1967   *The Biological Foundations of Language.* New York: John Wiley.

Long, Michael H.

1995   The least a second language acquisition theory needs to explain. In: H. Douglas Brown and Susan Gonzo (eds.), *Readings on Second Language Acquisition*, 470-490. Englewood Cliffs: Prentice Hall.

Lozanov, Georgi

1979   *Suggestology and Outline of Suggestopedy.* New York: Gordon and Breach.

Ludwig, J. M.

1979   The cognitive method and error analysis. *Foreign Language Annals* 12: 209-212.

Lugton, R. (ed.)

1971   *Toward a Cognitive Approach to Second Language Acquisition.* Philadelphia: Center for Curriculum Development.

Maiguascha, Raffaella

1984   Semantic fields: towards a methodology for teaching vocabulary in the L2 classroom. *Canadian Modern Language Review* 40: 274-97.

1989   Il linguaggio figurato nella didattica dell'italiano come lingua seconda: una proposta metodologica. In: A. N. Mancini and P. Giordano (eds), *Italiana 1987*, 36-35. River Forest: Rosary College.

McArthur, T.

1984   *A Foundation Course for Language Teachers.* Cambridge: Cambridge University Press.

McKay, S. L.

1980   On notional syllabuses. *Modern Language Journal* 64: 179-186.

1985   *Teaching Grammar.* Oxford: Pergamon.

McLaughlin, B.

1987   *Theories of Second-Language Learning.* London: Edward Arnold.

McNeill, David

1987   *Psycholinguistics: A New Approach.* New York: Harper and Row.

1992   *Hand and Mind: What Gestures Reveal about Thought.* Chicago: University of Chicago Press.

Meystell, Alexander

1995   *Semiotic Modeling and Situation Analysis: An Introduction.* Bala Cynwyd, Pennsylvania.: AdRem.

Mignault, Louis B.

   1978   Suggestopedia: Is there a better way to learn? *Canadian Modern Language Review* 34: 695-701.

Miller, George A. and P. M. Gildea

   1991   How children learn words. In: S-Y Wand (ed.), *The Emergence of Language: Development and Evolution.*, 150-158. New York: W.H. Freeman.

Mohan, B. A.

   1986   *Language and Content.* Reading, Mass.: Addison-Wesley.

Morris, Charles

   1938   *Foundations of the Theory of Signs.* Chicago: University of Chicago Press.

   1946   *Writings on the General Theory of Signs.* The Hague: Mouton.

Morris, Desmond

   1979   *Gestures: Their Origins and Distributions.* London: Cape.

Musumeci, Diane

   1997   *Breaking Tradition: An Exploration of the Historical Relationship between Theory and Practice in Second Language Teaching.* New York: McGraw-Hill.

Nation, I. S. P.

   1990   *Teaching and Learning Vocabulary.* Boston: Heinle and Heinle.

Neisser, Ulric (ed.)

   1987   *Concepts and Conceptual Development: Ecological and Intellectual Factors in Categorization.* Cambridge: Cambridge University Press.

Nelson, Katherine

   1996   *Language in Cognitive Development: The Emergence of the Mediated Mind.* Cambridge: Cambridge University Press.

Nemser, W.

   1971   Approximative systems of foreign language learners. *International Review of Applied Linguistics* 9: 115-123.

Newmark, L. and B. Reibel

   1966   Necessity and sufficiency in language learning. *International Review of Applied Linguistics* 40: 157-165.

Nöth, Winfred

   1990   *Handbook of Semiotics.* Bloomington: Indiana University Press.

Nuessel, Frank and Caterina Cicogna

    1992   Pedagogical applications of the bimodal model of learning through visual and auditory stimuli. *Romance Languages Annual* 3: 289-292.

    1993   Narrative texts and images in the teaching of the Italian language and Italian culture. *Romance Languages Annual* 4: 319-324.

O'Malley, J. M. and A. U. Chamot

    1990   *Learning Strategies in Second Language Acquisition.* Cambridge: Cambridge University Press.

Ogden, C. K. and I. A. Richards

    1923   *The Meaning of Meaning.* London: Routledge and Kegan Paul.

Oller, John W.

    1993   *Methods that Work: Ideas for Literacy and Language Teachers.* Boston: Heinle and Heinle.

Omaggio, Alice

    1986   *Teaching Language in Context.* Boston: Heinle and Heinle.

Opie, I. and P. Opie

    1959   *The Lore and Language of Schoolchildren.* Frogmore: Paladin.

Ortony, Andrew (ed.)

    1979   *Metaphor and Thought.* Cambridge: Cambridge University Press.

Osgood, Charles E. and Thomas A. Sebeok (eds.)

    1954   *Psycholinguistics: A Survey of Theory and Research Problems.* Baltimore: Waverley Press.

Palmer, Harold

    1917   *The Scientific Teaching and Study of Languages.* Yonkers-on-Hudson: World Book.

    1921   *The Oral Method of Teaching Languages.* Cambridge: Heffer.

    1922   *The Principles of Language-Study.* Oxford: Oxford University Press.

Patterson, C. H.

    1973   *Humanistic Education.* New Jersey: Prentice-Hall.

Peal, Elisabeth and Wallace E. Lambert

    1962   The relation of bilingualism to intelligence. *Psychological Monographs* 76, Entire Issue.

Peirce, Charles S.

    1931-1958 *Collected Papers.* Cambridge: Harvard University Press.

Piaget, Jean

1969   *The Child's Conception of the World*. Totowa: Littlefield, Adams and Company.

Pinker, Stephen

1990   Language acquisition. In: D. N. Osherson and H. Lasnik (eds.), *Language: An Invitation to Cognitive Science*, 191-241. Cambridge: MIT Press.

Piper, D.

1985   Contrastive rhetoric and reading in second language: Theoretical perspectives on classroom practice. *Canadian Modern Language Review* 42: 34-43.

Pollio, H., J. Barrow, H. Fine, and M. Pollio

1977   *Psychology and the Poetics of Growth: Figurative Language in Psychology, Psychotherapy, and Education*. Hillsdale, NJ: Lawrence Erlbaum Associates.

Porcelli, Gianfranco

1994   *Principi di glottodidattica*. Brescia: Editrice La Scuola.

Poyatos, F.

1989   Nonverbal communication in foreign-language teaching and learning: A theoretical and methodological approach. In: A. Helbo (ed.), *Evaluation and Language Teaching*, 45-59. Frankfurt: Peter Lang.

Propp, Vladimir J.

1928   *Morphology of the Folktale*. Austin: University of Texas Press.

Raffler-Engel, Walburga von

1980   Kinesics and paralinguistics: A neglected factor in second-language research and teaching. *Canadian Modern Language Review* 36: 1980: 225-237.

Ramírez, Arnulfo

1995   *Creating Context for Second Language Acquisition: Theory and Methods*. New York: Longman.

Rauch, Irmengard

1999   *Semiotic Insights: The Data Do the Talking*. Toronto: University of Toronto Press.

Rector, M. and A. R. Trinta

1985   *Comunicação não verbal: A gestualidade Brazileira*. Petropolis: Editor Vozes.

Richards, I. A.

1936   *The Philosophy of Rhetoric*. Oxford: Oxford University Press.

Richards, Jack C. (ed.)

1974   *Error Analysis: Perspectives on Second Language Acquisition*. London: Longman.

1978   *Second Language Acquisition*. Rowley, Mass.: Newbury House.

Richards, Jack C. and Theodore S. Rodgers

1986   *Approaches and Methods in Language Teaching: A Description and Analysis*. Cambridge: Cambridge University Press.

Rivers, Wilga

1964   *The Psychologist and the Foreign Language Teacher*. Chicago: University of Chicago Press.

1983   *Communicating Naturally in a Second Language. Theory and Practice in Language Teaching*. Cambridge: Cambridge University Press.

Robinett, B. W. and J. Schachter (eds.)

1983   *Second Language Learning: Contrastive Analysis, Error Analysis and Related Aspects*. Ann Arbor: University of Michigan Press.

Rogers, Carl

1951   *Client-Centered Therapy*. Boston: Houghton Mifflin.

1961   *On Becoming a Person: A Therapist's View of Psychotherapy*. Boston: Houghton Mifflin.

Rosch Eleanor

1973a   On the internal structure of perceptual and semantic categories. In: T. E. Moore (ed.), *Cognitive Development and Acquisition of Language.*, 111-144. New York: Academic.

1973b   Natural categories. *Cognitive Psychology* 4: 328-350.

1975a   Cognitive reference points. *Cognitive Psychology* 7: 532-547.

1975b   Cognitive representations of semantic categories. *Journal of Experimental Psychology* 104: 192-233.

Russo, Gerald A.

1997   *A Conceptual Fluency Framework for the Teaching of Italian as a Second Language*. University of Toronto, Dissertation.

Sapir, Edward

1921   *Language*. New York: Harcourt, Brace, and World.

Saussure, Ferdinand de

1916   *Cours de linguistique générale*. Paris: Payot.

Savignon, Sandra J.

  1992   Problem solving and the negotiation of meaning. In: C. Cicogna, M. Danesi, and A. Mollica (eds.), *Problem Solving in Second Language Teaching*, 11-25. Welland: Le Soleil.

Scherer, G. A. C. and M. Wertheimer

  1964   *A Psycholinguistic Experiment in Foreign-Language Teaching*. New York: McGraw-Hill.

Schogt, Henry

  1988   *Linguistics, Literary Analysis, and Literary Translation*. Toronto: University of Toronto Press.

Schulz, Renate A.

  1986   From achievement to proficiency through classroom instruction: Some caveats. *Modern Language Journal* 70: 373-379

Scovel, Thomas

  1988   *A Time to Speak: A Psycholinguistic Inquiry into the Critical Period for Human Speech*. Rowley, Mass.: Newbury House.

Scovel, Thomas

  1998   *Psycholinguistics*. Oxford: Oxford University Press.

Searle, John R.

  1969   *Speech Acts: An Essay in the Philosophy of Language*. Cambridge: Cambridge University Press.

Sebeok, Thomas A.

  1976   *Contributions to the Doctrine of Signs*. Lanham: University Press of America.

  1979   *The Sign and Its Masters*. Austin: University of Texas Press.

  1981   *The Play of Musement*. Bloomington: Indiana University Press.

  1986   *I Think I Am a Verb: More Contributions to the Doctrine of Signs*. New York: Plenum.

  1991   *A Sign is Just a Sign*. Bloomington: Indiana University Press.

  1994   *Signs: An Introduction to Semiotics*. Toronto: University of Toronto Press.

Sebeok, Thomas A. and Marcel Danesi

  2000   *The Forms of Meaning: Modeling Systems Theory and Semiotics*. Berlin: Mouton de Gruyter.

Seedhouse, Paul

    1994   Linking pedagogical purpose to linguistic patterns of interaction: the analysis of communication in the language classroom. *International Review of Applied Linguistics* 32: 303-320.

Seliger, H.

    1978   Implications of a multiple critical periods hypothesis for second language learning. In: W. Ritchie (ed.), *Second language acquisition research*, 21-35. New York: Academic.

Selinker, Larry

    1972   Interlanguage. *International Review of Applied Linguistics* 10: 209-231.

Shibles, W.

    1989   How German vocabulary pictures emotion. *British Journal of Language Teaching* 27: 141.

Shrum, J. L. and E. W. Glisan

    1994   *Contextualized Language Instruction*. Boston: Heinle and Heinle.

Singleton, D.

    1989   *Language Acquisition: The Age Factor*. Clevedon: Multilingual Matters.

Skinner, B. F.

    1957   *Verbal Behavior*. New York: Appleton-Century-Crofts.

Smith, P. D.

    1970   *A Comparison of the Cognitive and Audio-Lingual Approaches to Foreign Language Instruction*. Philadelphia: Center for Curriculum Development.

Sontag, Susan

    1978   *Illness as Metaphor*. New York: Farrar, Straus and Giroux.

Sperry, Roger W.

    1968   Hemisphere disconnection and unity in conscious awareness. *American Psychologist* 23: 723-733.

Spolsky, Bernard

    1989   *Conditions for Second Language Learning*. Oxford: Oxford University Press.

    1998   *Sociolinguistics*. Oxford: Oxford University Press.

Sridhar, S. N

   1981   Contrastive analysis, error analysis and interlanguage: Three phases of one goal. In: J. Fisiak (ed.), *Contrastive Linguistics and the Language Teacher*, 207-241. Oxford: Pergamon.

Stern, H. H.

   1983   *Fundamental Concepts of Language Teaching*. Oxford: Oxford University Press.

Stevick, Earl W.

   1976   *Memory, Meaning and Method. Some Psychological Perspectives on Language Learning*. Rowley Mass.: Newbury House Publishers.

   1980   *Teaching Language. A Way and Ways*. Rowley Mass.: Newbury House Publishers.

   1990   *Humanism in Language Teaching*. Oxford: Oxford University Press.

Stockwell, Robert P., Donald J. Bowen, and John W. Martin

   1965a   *The Sounds of English and Spanish*. Chicago: University of Chicago Press.

   1965b   *The Grammatical Structures of English and Spanish*. Chicago: University of Chicago Press.

Sweet, Henry

   1899   *The Practical Study of Languages: A Guide for Teachers and Learners*. London: J. M. Dent & Sons.

Sweetser, Eve

   1990   *From Etymology to Pragmatics: The Mind-as-Body Metaphor in Semantic Structure and Semantic Change*. Cambridge: Cambridge University Press.

Tannen, Deborah

   1989   *Talking Voices*. Cambridge: Cambridge University Press.

Taylor, John R.

   1995   *Linguistic Categorization: Prototypes in Linguistic Theory*. Oxford: Oxford University Press.

Terrell, Tracy D.

   1991   The role of grammar instruction in a communicative approach. *Modern Language Journal* 75: 52-63.

Titone, Renzo

   1968   *Teaching Foreign Languages: An Historical Sketch*. Washington, D. C.: Georgetown University Press.

Titone, Renzo and Marcel Danesi

    1985   *Applied Psycholinguistics: An Introduction to the Psychology of Second Language Learning and Teaching*. Toronto: University of Toronto Press.

Valdman, Albert

    1975   Error analysis and grading in the preparation of teaching material. *The Modern Language Journal* 59: 422-426.

Van Ek, J. A.

    1975   *The Threshold Level in a European Unit/Credit System for Modern Language Teaching by Adults*. Strasbourg: Council of Europe.

Vygotsky, Lev S.

    1962   *Thought and Language*. Cambridge, Mass.: MIT Press.

    1978   *Mind in Society*. Cambridge, Mass.: Cambridge University Press.

Wardhaugh, Ronald

    1970   The contrastive analysis hypothesis. *TESOL Quarterly* 4: 123-130.

Wells, G.

    1986   *The Meaning Makers: Children Learning Language and Using Language to Learn*. Portsmouth: Heinemann.

Wernicke, Carl

1874   *Der aphasische Symptomenkomplex*. Breslau: Cohn and Weigart.

White, L.

    1990   Second language acquisition and universal grammar. *Studies in Second Language Acquisition* 12: 121-133.

Whorf, Benjamin L.

    1956   *Language, Thought and Reality*. Cambridge, Mass.: MIT Press.

Widdowson, H. G

    1972   *Teaching Language as Communication*. Oxford: Oxford University Press.

Wilkins, D. A.

    1976   *Notional Syllabuses*. Oxford: Oxford University Press.

Wolff, Dieter

    1987   Some assumptions about second language text comprehension. *Studies in Second Language Acquisition* 9: 307-326.

Index

acquisition by stages, 16

addressee, 91

addresser, 91

anaphora, 90

antonym, 88

applied semiotics, 22, 157-167

argument, 30

Aristotle, 25, 136-137

Army specialized training program, 7

association, 51, 136-137

association-by-inference, 51-52, 56, 136

association-by-sense, 51, 136

audiolingual method, 7-8

audiovisual method, 7-8

Barthes, Roland, 27,

basic concept, 44

behaviorism, 7

Blade Runner, 115

brain, 18-20

cataphora, 90

circuits, 45-46

code, 36-37, 91

cognitive mode, 147-148

cognitive-code method, 8

cognitivism, 8

color terms, 21-22, 33-35, 77-79, 131-133

Comenius, 3-4

communicative competence, 9

communicative language teaching, 9-10

communicative syllabus, 10

community counseling, 11

conative, 93

concept, 31, 43-44, 73-74

conceptual fluency, 13-14

conceptual knowing, 15

conceptual metaphor, 54-56, 138-139

conceptual metonym, 149

conceptual reorganization, 35, 39-40, 75

conceptual structure, 13

connotation, 50-51, 108-134

connotative chaining, 110-111

connotative concept, 110-113

connotative network, 50-51

consistency, 128-129

contact, 91

context, 90-91

contrastive analysis, 7-8, 105-107

crisscrossing, 53

critical period, 20-21

deductive method, 3

denotation, 48-59, 77-107

denotative concept, 77, 81-85

denotative network, 77-78, 48-49 84

dicisign, 30

direct method, 2, 3-5

discourse, 90-101, 119-123, 135-136, 138